t.f.h.

the marine aquarium
in theory and practice

by dr. c. w. emmens

Title page photo:
Marine community tank. Shown are a surgeon fish (partly hidden), *Zebrasoma xanthurus*, and two butterfly-fishes, *Chaetodon semilarvatus* and *Heniochus acuminatus* (to the left). Photo by Guy van den Bossche.

Photos by M. Goto are from the Japanese book *Marine Life Documents*, text and photos by Michio Goto, published by Kodansha, Ltd.

ISBN 0-87666-446-X

Distributed in the U.S. by T.F.H. Publications, Inc., 211 West Sylvania Avenue, PO Box 427, Neptune, NJ 07753; in England by T.F.H. (Gt. Britain) Ltd., 13 Nutley Lane, Reigate, Surrey; in Canada to the pet trade by Rolf C. Hagen Ltd., 3225 Sartelon Street, Montreal 382, Quebec; in Canada to the book trade by H & L Pet Supplies, Inc., 27 Kingston Crescent, Kitchener, Ontario N28 2T6; in Southeast Asia by Y.W. Ong, 9 Lorong 36 Geylang, Singapore 14; in Australia and the South Pacific by Pet Imports Pty. Ltd., P.O. Box 149, Brookvale 2100, N.S.W. Australia; in South Africa by Valid Agencies, P.O. Box 51901, Randburg 2125 South Africa. Published by T.F.H. Publications, Inc., Ltd., the British Crown Colony of Hong Kong.

CONTENTS

Underwater coral reef in the Ryukyus. These corals are not completely exposed to air during low tide except those found near the surface. Photo by M. Goto.

This book is not intended for the complete beginner in fish keeping, but for someone already familiar with the elements of aquarium management. In many ways it could be regarded as a conversion course for fresh-water aquarists, but it goes beyond that, and discusses the most up-to-date information on marine aquaria on the level of the advanced aquarist in that field.

Familiarity with air-stones, filters and heaters, etc. is assumed, although these are further discussed in relation to salt water aquarium keeping. The result is a series of essays on vital topics for the marine aquarist, such as the real function of biological filters, the changes which captive sea water undergoes in the tank and their significance to the hobbyist, the maintenance of health in the salt water tank and the treatment of disease when it occurs.

The author never takes an inflexible attitude, and recognizes that we are still so ignorant of many factors that it would be foolish to assert that any one method is correct or even the best where marine aquaria are concerned. We are all explorers in the field and should hope to make significant contributions to successful salt water aquarium-keeping for many years to come, or at least to be receptive to the ideas and findings of those who do so. The fascinating possibilities of marine fish breeding are only just beginning to become realities—think how long it may be before we can raise tank-bred marines as we do fresh-water species.

Sincere thanks are due to various correspondents too numerous for individual mention, to members of the Marine Aquarium Research Institute of Australia, and by no means least to Dr. Axelrod and his staff, who as always, turn a bare manuscript into an attractive book.

C. W. Emmens

Clown trigger, *Balistoides niger*. The rather rare blue-spotted variety is particularly attractive. Photo by K. Paysan.

Chapter I

The Tank and Equipment

INTRODUCTION

Marine fish-keeping has made tremendous strides in the last few years, and salt-water aquaria are now being kept with a high degree of success in the home and office. Probably, the success rate is now approaching that of the fresh-water aquarist, and any experienced hobbyist can certainly keep marine tanks going more successfully than his relatively inexperienced fresh-water counterpart. However, it is only by alertness and intelligent care that he can do this; lack of observation and reasonable information about the hobby will lead to dismal failure in many instances. The raw beginner is advised to start under expert guidance—if he can get it—with selected "tough" fishes in the first instance, and with as large a tank as he can afford, relatively few fishes, and a fairly simple set-up which can be elaborated as experience is gained. However a start is made, the beginner is in difficulties because of his inexperience and because any new tank undergoes a settling down period during which more is likely to go wrong than at any other time in the future. He is thus doubly handicapped, and it is a tribute to modern texts and equipment that so many are now succeeding where so few did so only a short time ago.

Keeping salt water tanks is a fascinating hobby—there is so much to experiment with and to learn, so that although we can expect to manage our "show" tank or tanks successfully and to enjoy them without undue labor, there is also open to us an endless field for experiment if we are willing to spend the time and take the risk of at least occasional failures. In addition to the keeping of fishes, a vast world of invertebrates exists in the sea, many of which can be kept in small tanks, sometimes mixed with the fishes themselves, but often best kept alone. Breeding marine fishes and invertebrates, is also an almost unexplored territory for the aquarist, but one which is being gradually penetrated, so that in a few years' time we shall probably be succeeding with many species, rather than the mere handful of the present time. The complexity of the salt-water environment far exceeds that of the fresh-water lakes and rivers; the composition of sea-water, for instance, is imperfectly understood, and the importance of many of its components is unknown. Its storage and maintenance is also much more of a problem than with fresh water, as we shall see in the pages which follow.

Probably the most successful marine aquarists will be those who have never kept fresh-water fishes. This is because fresh-water enthusiasts are more likely to overcrowd the marine tank and to strive for a planted effect, and in general to try to manage their tanks in an inappropriate manner. Although much equipment is common to the two hobbies, its use in the marine tank is often quite different in principle and in effect from that in the fresh-water aquarium. There is also a greater variety

Lookdowns, *Selene vomer*, are best kept in tanks by themselves to avoid dorsal fin damage. If this is not possible, only non-aggressive species should be housed with them. Photo by Dr. H.R. Axelrod.

Smoothhead unicorn fish, *Naso lituratus*. Surgeons (*Acanthurus*, *Naso*, *Zebrasoma*, etc.) feed primarily on algae, but deep-frozen lettuce is a good substitute. Photo by K.H. Choo.

Schooling and open-ocean carangids like these *Pterocaesio diagramma* rarely do well in captivity, except possibly in large circular display tanks of some public aquariums. Photo by M. Goto.

of ways of managing salt-water tanks. It is quite possible to maintain them over a spectrum of conditions which range from the popular "sterile" system, with ultra-filtration of water and great care over bacterial and other contamination, to the "natural" system in which living coral, anemones and other invertebrates, algae and fishes are kept together in a single community. The author doesn't like the use of inverted commas, but neither the word "sterile" nor the word "natural" really describes the conditions in such tanks; they merely contrast different sets of basic principles, both of which can be made to work. The "sterile" tank is by no means sterile, and the "natural" one by no means natural. In fact, no tank, however large, can maintain conditions very much resembling the ocean for any length of time.

In the majority of cases, marine tanks will have to be filled with artificial salt water, at best with a small percentage of natural sea water. This is becoming less of a difficulty as good mixes become available and the natural

article more and more polluted. Even those who live by the sea are finding it increasingly difficult to collect acceptable water without travelling well out into the ocean to get it. Much coastal water is so polluted that a good artificial mix is far to be preferred. There are also tablets available now to keep up a supply of trace elements in the tank. Feeding must usually be unlike that to which the fishes have been accustomed, and many fishes have to learn to eat the foods available and to feed at intervals from the top of the water, or in mid-water, rather than from the bottom, in a steady browsing. How well they do this often depends on how they have been collected and treated before reaching the aquarist, who regrettably cannot always be blamed for failure with poorly handled specimens prior to sale. What he can do is to learn how to pick the really bad ones and leave them strictly alone, and to find a reliable dealer who takes pride in his work, knows where to buy his fishes, and takes a helpful interest in his customers.

Typical tropical brackish water area. Water from most coastal regions is often unsafe, particularly if situated near human habitations and farms. Photo by Dr. H.R. Axelrod.

Top: target fish, *Therapon jarbua*. Bottom: monos, *Monodactylus argenteus*. Both species are adaptable to brackish fresh water and even hard alkaline fresh water having a high calcium content. Photo by G. Senfft.

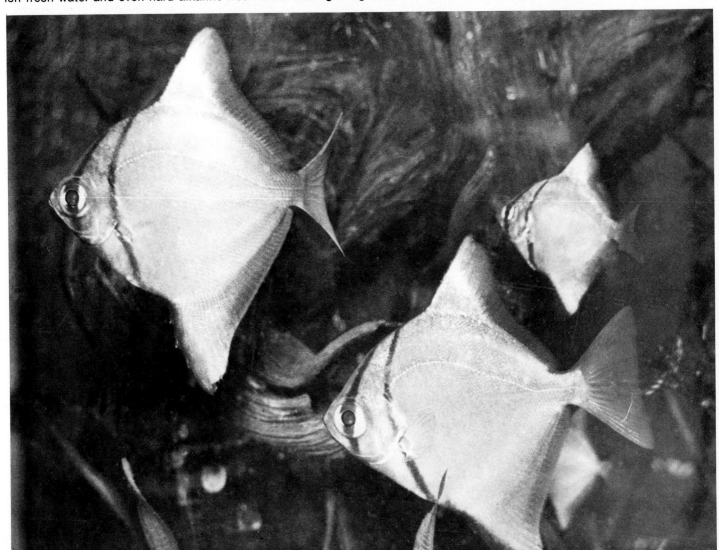

Short bigeye, *Pristigenys altus.* This is a juvenile taken from very shallow water (less than a foot) in one of the inlets in New Jersey. Adults are found in deeper water. Photo by A. Norman.

During the summer months it is possible to collect some tropical species as far north as the coast of New Jersey shown here. The man-made jetty is for the control of beach erosion. Photo by Dr. H.R. Axelrod.

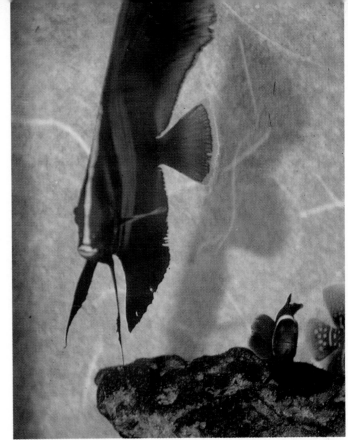

The batfish *Platax pinnatus*.
Keep this species as the
dominant fish of a tank or fins
will be ripped. The colors fade as
the fish grows; it is a rather
delicate species while young.
Photo by R. Zukal.

Platax pinnatus (adult)...
greedy, fast-growing and tough.
Photo by Dr. G.R. Allen at
Euston Reef, Great Barrier Reef,
Australia.

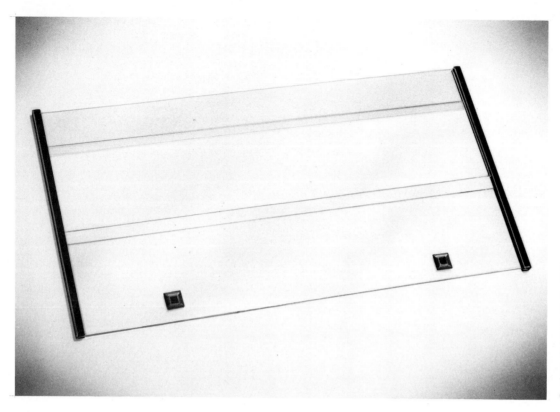

A well constructed tank cover is a good investment. It serves as a barrier to jumping fish and minimizes rapid loss of water through evaporation.

THE TANK

Salt-water attacks metal, aquarium cement, various plastics and a host of other materials unaffected or little affected by fresh-water. The material of a marine tank is therefore critical and it must be guaranteed against corrosion. It is rarely satisfactory to line a tank with protective material such as fiber glass or silicone cement, as adhesion can frequently break down and trouble commence. Nylon coated tanks, apparently made by dipping the whole tank in a suitable solution, were once on the market but seem to have disappeared.

A marine tank must therefore be made of glass and first quality stainless steel, a suitable plastic, solely of glass, or with a glass panel or panels bonded into inert material such as fiber glass, cement or wood, although wooden tanks are rarely suitable, except for outdoor use. All-glass tanks are undoubtedly the most elegant, and can now be made to any desirable shape or size. They are non-toxic, relatively inexpensive, but must be carefully seated in order to avoid a cracked base. Make sure that any all-glass tank you purchase is geometrically true, check the stand or surface on which you are

going to put the tank for absence of tilt, and then place a $\frac{1}{2}''$ layer of styrofoam or some other suitable compressible material to absorb any residual lack of fit of the tank to the stand. This layer should be firm, but able to give sufficiently to take up the fit. It should be cut exactly to fit the tank base or very slightly overlap it, as it is most important that it is present under the outside edges, so that the vertical glass is adequately supported.

With an all-glass tank, it is easy to construct the most suitable type of top cover. All but the smallest tanks need support across the top, done by inserting a permanent brace of glass in the center on a level with the top edges, but all other glass fits into the top and sits on flanges cemented about $\frac{1}{2}''$ below the top edges, so that drip-back occurs completely within the tank. Suitable gaps or holes can be arranged for the admission of air-lines and feeding. These arrangements ensure minimum top splash or creeping of salt and make maintenance a lot easier than with most other types of tank.

A normal exhibition tank should be as large as you can manage to have. Remember that

Different shapes of tanks other than the conventional rectangular shape are now available commercially, although they may cost a little bit more. Courtesy of O'Dell Manufacturing Co.

15

A 100-gallon tank, fully set up, could weigh more than a thousand pounds, so the means by which such a tank would be supported is important. Mr Warren Tom of Honolulu, Hawaii, shown here, utiliz-ed large concrete blocks to support his marine tank. Metal-framed marine aquaria like the one shown here have been replaced in almost every case by all-glass aquaria; the all-glass tanks are lighter and eliminate the danger of salt-to-metal contact. Photo by Dr. Herbert R. Axelrod.

Large display tanks typically seen in many public aquariums. Both these tanks exhibit coral reef fishes from the Pacific. Photos by Dr. H.R. Axelrod.

Aeration and electrical apparatus for this custom-made marine tank are conveniently concealed behind the wall. Photo by Dr. H.R. Axelrod.

water weighs a lot, each U.S. gallon is $8\frac{1}{4}$ lb in weight, and the floor below must be able to support it. With normal house constructions, this does not start to matter with less than 4ft to 5ft tanks (in length), and large tanks are in order as long as they are not very broad and deep—up to $18'' \times 18''$ in cross section would usually be safe. Otherwise check carefully where the tank is put and take professional advice with tanks larger than indicated. With a large tank, many problems that would otherwise arise are minimized right from the start, and as there are going to be enough without asking for more, it pays to heed this advice.

Tanks of less than about 25 gallons (just under 90 liters) are difficult to maintain because the small water volume allows dangerous overheating in summer, unless in an air-conditioned room, can support few fishes without a lot of mechanical filtering and is liable to rapid changes in composition if anything is neglected or goes wrong. A power failure places the small tank in immediate danger, whereas a large tank will keep warm, assuming it to be a tropical one, as it usually will be, for many hours. Failure of pumps, filters, aerators, etc. in a large tank that is not overcrowded does not mean immediate disaster, nor does a minor degree of overfeeding, the undetected death of a small fish, and many other events which can upset a small tank very quickly. It is not even significantly cheaper to install a small tank, except for the cost of the fishes. Equipment for marine aquaria costs much more than the tanks themselves, which are frequently the cheapest item, costing less than a single fish might! Thus, a marine tank may cost less than the stand on which it sits, the pump and filters it needs, the artificial salt-water it probably contains, and any single fish it holds.

LIGHTING

Practically all indoor aquaria need a top light which sits over the cover glasses and is protected from splash or condensation by them. The cover glass or glasses are thus very necessary; as well as preventing fishes from jumping out, they stop unwanted material from falling in, and make the electrical equipment over them safe to install. The top light is usually under a hood of reflecting material, most often stainless steel or plastic. It should clear the cover glass by at least $\frac{1}{2}''$, and looks best if it fits snugly along the length of the tank. It may be incandescent or fluorescent, most often the latter. The importance of adequate lighting is to maintain algal growth at a suitable level, to enable fish to feed, and not least, to enable the owner to see them. Its nature is therefore critical, and we shall now discuss it.

By far the most popular is fluorescent lighting, of which a range is available specially for aquarium use. Manufacturers try to aim at the best combinations of efficiency and color; the latter is always subject in part to consumer preference, but the lighting must support algal growth unless the aquarist aims at a completely "sterile" tank. Fluorescent tubes give off bands of monochromatic light, single wave-lengths scattered here and there across the spectrum, instead of the continuous spectrum of daylight or of incandescent lighting. This is no disadvantage as long as bands exist in the right areas for plant growth—mainly the red end of the spectrum, and for acceptable viewing—more towards the blue end of the spectrum. So called "daylight" tubes are rather poor in plant stimulating areas, but "white" or "warm white" and similar tubes are better and also give for most people a preferable appearance. Special tubes such as the "Grolux" series give reddish, violet or more natural looking light

Fluorescent bulbs housed in reflectors are the most popular type of lighting unit for marine tanks. In addition to lasting longer than incandescent bulbs, fluorescent bulbs also provide more lighting power per unit of wattage consumed, and they throw off less heat than incandescent bulbs.

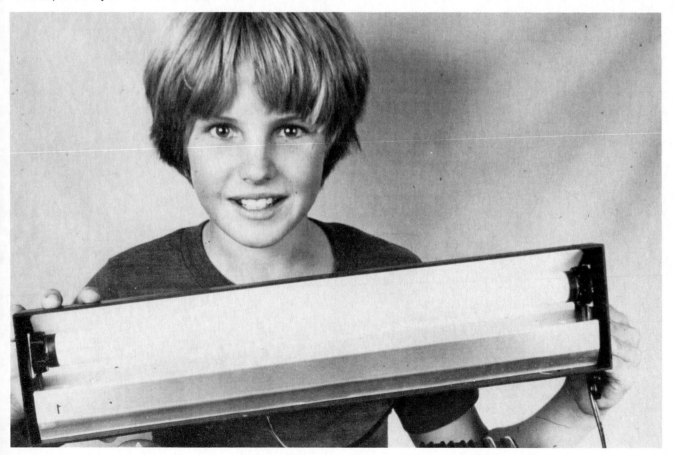

Night-time and day-time color patterns in butterflyfishes. Upper row: day-time. Bottom row: night-time. Photos by M. Goto.

Chaetodon plebeius

Chaetodon trifascialis

Chaetodon auripes

Chaetodon auriga

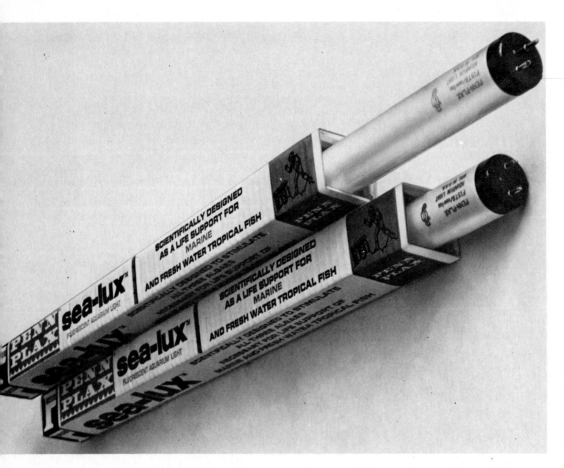

Presumably all three types of algae are stimulated by these fluorescent lamps on the basis that each bulb covers the whole light spectrum. Courtesy of Penn-Plax Plastics.

and are especially designed to stimulate plant growth. Other colors may be chosen by the aquarist for their interesting effects on the look of the fishes and decorations. Combinations of tubes may be used over large tanks.

Within reasonable limits, the total illumination per day is what determines plant growth. We shall see elsewhere that algae other than one-celled varieties are difficult to maintain in the salt tank, and what is wanted is usually green algae. Insufficient light stimulates the growth of brown, unsightly coats of algae over the tank glass and contents. With the average fluorescent tube, 20 to 30 watts for 12–18 hours per day is adequate for tanks of 30–60 gallons, rising to 40 watts or even more for larger and deeper tanks. Less than 12 hours of illumination per day, unless some natural daylight falls on the tank, is not sufficient, because the fishes must be able to see and feed.

The position of the lights over the tank is also important. Front lighting, with the top light towards the front of the tank, gives best illumin-ation of the inhabitants but stimulates algal growth on the front glass, which will need fre-quent cleaning. Placing the light towards the back of the tank causes algal growth to be greatest where it is wanted—on back and side glasses, coral, rocks, etc., and gives the best general tank appearance but is less helpful for viewing the fishes, which tend to be shadowed by the light instead of it showing up the brilliant colors. Perhaps the best solution is a mid-top light or one in a hood so constructed that it cuts off light tending to fall obliquely on the front glass. Alternatively, you can shift the light for viewing but keep it routinely more to-wards the back—not, perhaps, a very satis-factory solution!

Fluorescent lights are relatively cool and much more efficient than incandescent lights. Although most aquarists prefer the appear-ance of ordinary incandescent lighting, it has to be admitted that it may give problems of overheating in warm weather, and has to be kept clearer of the top glass because of the danger of cracking if the bulbs are nearer than, say, $\frac{1}{2}''$. When purchasing a top light, ask your dealer to point out various types of illumination and if possible try them out over a tank of fishes so that you can see the different effects. Remember that salt water plus electricity spells acute danger of shorts, corrosion and even electric shocks, and see that any tank-lighting combination gives full protection against spray, splashing and creep of salt. Inspect the interior of top lights occasionally to check on their condition.

HEATING

The tropical marine tank needs a temperature of 70° to 85°F (21°–30°C) preferably towards the middle of that range. About 76° or 78°F (25°C) is good for most fishes, but there are exceptions. This will usually be warmer than the average living room and much warmer than night-time temperatures without air-conditioning or heating in many parts of the globe. Your dealer will advise on the best wattage for your particular circumstances, the aim being to have adequate but not excessive heating. Excessive heating capacity means that the thermostat controlling the heater(s) is clicking on and off frequently and may show early wear, with the danger of malfunction. Then, if for instance it stays on when it should have gone off, the excess heating capacity will cook the tank contents. With an adequate heating capacity only, a dangerous rise in temperature may be avoided. If the heating fails, nothing will save a small tank in a cold room, but a large tank of 50 gallons or more will take a long time to cool down to a dangerous level and so remedial measures are usually possible.

There are numerous heaters available besides those illustrated here. Heaters vary from types that are attached vertically or horizontally to even completely submersible types. Courtesy of Ebo-Jager, Inc. and Penn-Plax Plastics, Inc.

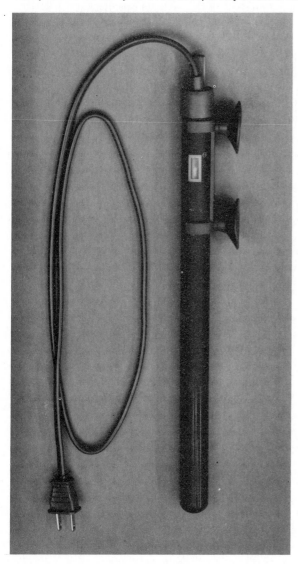
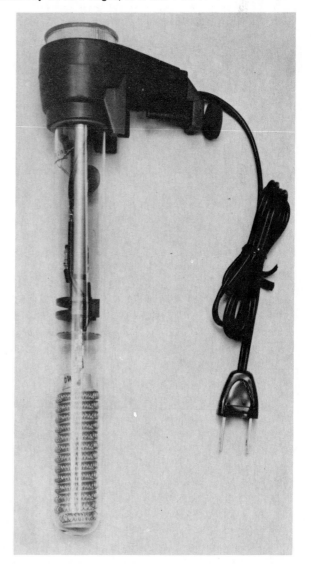

Left: the hogfish, *Bodianus loxozonus*. Right: two-banded grouper, *Diploprion bifasciatum*. These species are carnivorous, so small fishes and invertebrates should not be kept along with them. Photos by M. Goto.

Royal empress angel, *Pygoplites diacanthus*, a difficult fish to keep. It usually pecks at food at best and gradually starves to death. Photo by M. Goto.

Long-jawed squirrelfish, *Adioryx spinifer*. This species is nocturnal, spending more time behind the rocks than swimming in the open areas of the tank. Photo by M. Goto.

A grouper, *Plectropomus* sp., also known as rock cod and an important food fish in many places. In some areas of the world specimens may be toxic and cause ciguatera disease (ciguatera poisoning). Photo by M. Goto.

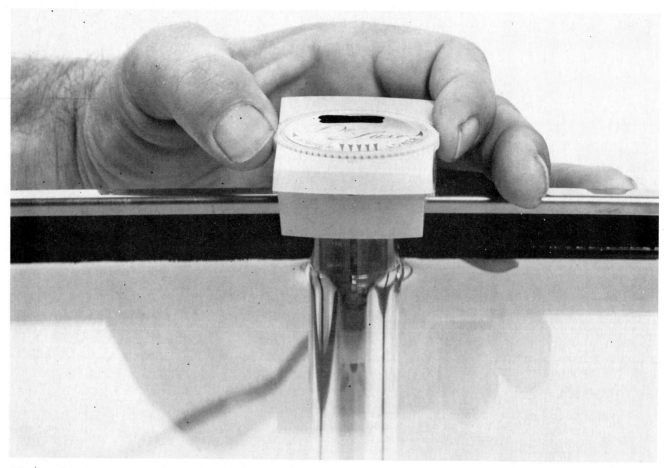

A heater should have the temperature control within view and should be equipped with a pilot light or warning device for greater safety. Photo by H. Radin & Associates.

Always install a thermometer so that a glance will tell you if all is well, but in addition, use a pilot light if possible, often built into the thermostat, which tells you when it is on. A thermostat perpetually turned on in a tank which goes on cooling down shows heater failure, and so that source of trouble is rapidly apparent. Special resins which change color at different temperatures have been utilized as warning devices.

In a tank containing inhabitants from temperate climates, the usual problem is overheating in summer. This can be a real nuisance, as the heat capacity of water is very high, and cooling so slow in medium or larger sized tanks that the very effect wanted in tropical tanks can be dangerous in those needing cooler water. The tank mounts in temperature each day and may remain at a steady 80°–85°F (27°–30°C) far too warm for many of the creatures from

cooler seas. The only really satisfactory solution is refrigeration, which can be installed, or built in as an integral part of the tank. Such tanks are expensive but are commercially available for colleges, etc. Attempts to keep the aquarium cool with ice or ice packs are not usually successful as so much is needed. In many areas, therefore, a tropical marine tank is more likely to be successful than a cool tank which should be kept at perhaps 50°–60°F (10°–15°C).

Back to tropical tanks, if separate heaters and thermostats are to be used, it is best to install external thermostats with pilot lights, so that surveillance can be carried out as above. Otherwise, one of the various combinations can be used, preferably a completely submersible one hidden from view behind tank decorations, but not buried or liable to be buried, or it may fuse. It should also be clear of the side glasses, since direct contact could lead to a hot spot and possible cracking of the glass of the tank or heater. A drawback to submersible thermostats is that they cannot be altered without withdrawal from the water. Make sure that the equipment remains water tight if it is necessary to do this. In a fresh water tank, "layering" of the water may occur because the heated water rises and forms warm layers at the top, but in a marine tank the degree of aeration or its equivalent needed is such that adequate stirring occurs.

Some aquarists place the heater in the filter, which removes any danger of cracking the tank, or of layering, but adds the danger of boiling the water in the filter while the tank cools down, if anything goes wrong with the filter itself. On the whole, there would seem to be little point in doing this, even when filter construction allows it, and some degree of danger.

Others have experimented with cable heating, either inside or underneath the base of the tank. Although such a method sounds good, it has never caught on.

AERATION

In one form or another, aeration is essential in a marine aquarium. It is often combined with filtration, but even when it is, and additional aeration is perhaps unnecessary, many hobbyists like to see plenty of bubbles rising through the water and so put in extra air stones. This additional aeration rarely does any harm. In the fresh-water tank, it has been demonstrated that the main effect of aeration is to stir the water and to renew the surface layers so that a continuous interchange goes on between the water and the air above it. Short of such vigorous aeration that the tank would look

Aeration is easily regulated. It should be neither too strong, distressing the fish, nor too weak and therefore ineffectual. Photo by Dr. W. Klausewitz.

Octopuses, even large ones, are escape artists and should be kept in tanks with tight-fitting covers. Octopuses need large amounts of aeration. Photo by M. Goto.

A hermit crab (*Paguristes*) can be destructive and will prey on other animals. It is best not to include them in average tanks. Photo by Dr. K. Knaack.

Fiddler crabs (*Uca*) are intertidal animals and they need a soft bottom for burrowing. They can not be submerged all the time or they drown. Males wave their big claw to attract females and warn other males. Photo by Dr. H.R. Axelrod.

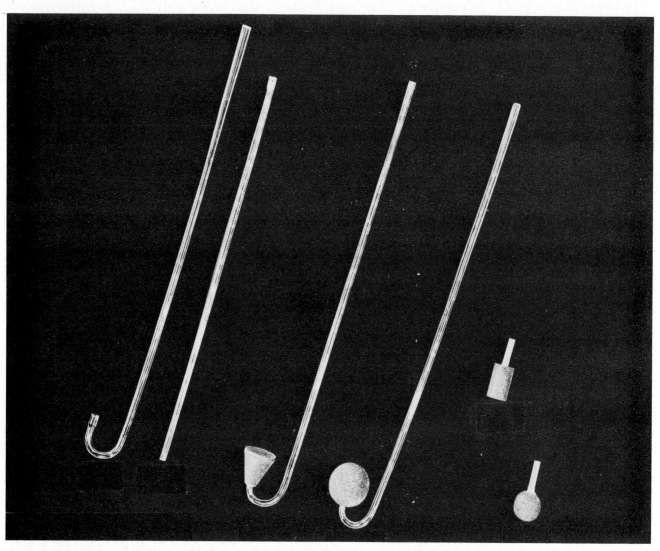
Various types of airstones and extensions are available in most pet shops.

like a boiling cauldron, most of the air-water exchange occurs at the surface, not between the bubbles and the water. It is thus possible, although not with any point to it, to "aerate" with pure nitrogen or even with carbon dioxide and to get benefit from it in the fresh-water aquarium. In an understocked, large sea-water tank, much the same probably holds, but the amount of stirring required, and thus the contribution of the bubbles themselves is to say the least greater than with the usual fresh-water setup.

It is thus more important, even with direct simple aeration, to get streams of fine bubbles into the water. Their stirring effect is greater too, as long as they are not extremely fine and form a mist, rather than a stream carrying water with it. Something like a bubble diameter of less than $\frac{1}{25}''$ (1 mm) is desirable, although

adequate experiments on this point still remain to be done. However, the marine tank will rather seldom have only simple aeration. It will usually be combined with filtration in one form or another, or with "protein" skimming and/or ozone addition, all of which are discussed later on. This means that water is circulated either within the tank or through external gadgetry in a more positive way, so that the lifting effect of simple air-stones is not the only consideration. The water is often returned to the tank at the surface, frequently in such a manner as to cause horizontal streaming and thus to accentuate the interchange at the air-water surface. In many a setup, practically the whole of the water in the tank may leave it and return each hour, so that much more effective mixing and surface interchange occurs than would happen with air-stones alone.

FILTRATION

In one form or another, filtration is almost mandatory in the marine aquarium. In this section, we are concerned more with the nature of equipment available than with its detailed functioning, and shall have a lot more to discuss later on. Filters are of several varieties and may perform several different services within the aquarium. These are mechanical removal of gross particles of material which otherwise cloud the water or collect in the tank, mechanical removal of fine as well as gross particles, chemical or physico-chemical removal of dissolved, unwanted toxins and waste products, and biological breakdown of either particulate or dissolved contaminants. The importance of the last-named in the marine tank has received poor recognition until recently.

The removal of gross particulate material such as uneaten food, feces and decayed material (even from dead fishes or their remains) is essential, or the water will become cloudy and smelly very rapidly. This is accomplished by simple physical filtration in an internal or external filter box with a layer or layers of glass wool, synthetic staple, or such-like. Very efficient filter pads are now available for this purpose. The area of such filters need not be great, and as they clog up they perform better and better until they are too clogged, when it is impossible to pass enough water through to do a good job of filtration. This may occur in a few days or a few weeks, in extreme instances a few months, in an understocked large tank with a big filter. When excess clogging occurs, the filter material has to be changed.

The removal of fine particulate matter (down to bacteria) is never adequately done by glass wool or pads; instead, specially made filter capsules or layers of diatomaceous earth, which is finely-packed diatom shells, must be

External filter box and pump. Courtesy Marineland Aquarium Products.

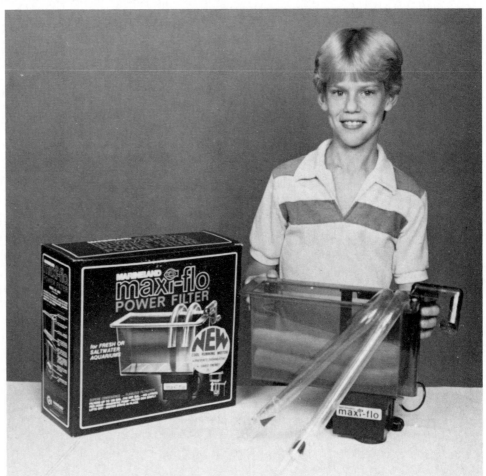

The sea anemone *Actinia tenebrosa*, found on the east coast of Australia. This anemone will accept a variety of food like small shrimps, crab meat, chopped clams, mussels, and fish. Photo by U.E. Friese.

Rough lima, *Lima scabra*. Scallops, which have eyes around their mantle, can be kept successfully for long periods. Photo by Dr. H.R. Axelrod.

A nudibranch like this *Chromodoris* sp. may not be easy to keep. Nudibranchs require foods similar to those eaten in the wild, and these foods are usually unknown or unavailable. Photo by Dr. H.R. Axelrod.

Filters like the ones shown are very useful for carrying activated charcoal to keep water clear. Photo by Dr. H.R. Axelrod.

used. Unless these filters are very large, the filtering material must usually be changed quite frequently—every few days is common—as they clog up rapidly. They produce beautifully clear water, and are normally served by a water pump, rather than an air lift of one kind or another. This is because considerable pressure is needed to force the water through the capsule, or through an adequate layer of fine diatomaceous earth, although the latter may be accomplished in a large set up by water pressure alone in a high column.

Chemical or physico-chemical methods fall into two main groups. In the first is activated carbon, or charcoal. This material, in the right condition, is able to absorb onto its surface all kinds of dissolved chemicals, even gases, to an almost miraculous extent. Finely divided and properly prepared, it can take up to 50% of its own weight of material. It will remove fine cloudiness, colored or smelly material, invisibly dissolved but dangerous toxic or obnoxious materials, metallic and other contaminants. It will also absorb vitamins, trace elements, disease cures and various other desirable elements, so it is not an unmixed blessing. Improperly prepared, it can change the pH of the water or even *donate* toxins if they have not been removed prior to its use. It thus requires careful washing in salt water before being placed in the filter, preferably by running a few gallons through it repeatedly for 24 hours before use. The so-called charcoal "coals," quite coarse in

size, are relatively useless and a danger in the tank. To be of any utility, pounds of them per medium-sized tank may be needed, and they may continue to give off unwanted substances for weeks. Instead, pin-head sized tiny granules are needed, which have an enormous surface per unit weight, when a few ounces will suffice. Naturally, they must be placed between layers of some other material to keep them in place.

Another set of compounds, the synthetic ion exchange resins, falls into the second group with activated charcoal. Their place in marine water filtration is open to discussion. In the fresh-water tank they may be used to remove heavy metals, even calcium, which means that they can be employed to soften the water or to take up unwanted metallic contaminants. They can also be used in combination or in series with each other to render the water virtually salt-free, better than many a grade of distilled water, but this is rarely needed. Usually, heavier metals are replaced by sodium, without serious disturbance of pH or changes in osmotic pressure. In the marine tank, everything is different. The resins will rapidly exchange all their sodium for calcium, magnesium, etc., of which there is so much present that little difference will be achieved. However, they will still absorb heavier metals, such as copper, and can be used to clean them out of a treated tank if they have been used in the attempted cure of disease. Naturally, they will also remove metallic trace elements, but they will not in

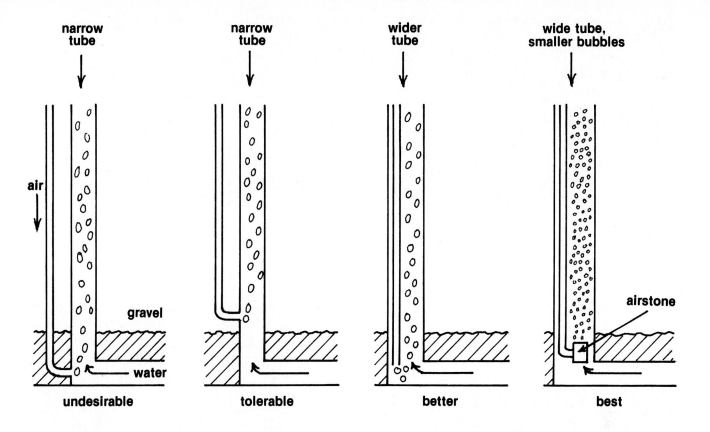

Different types of airlift and return tubes on undergravel filters with special reference to the position of air inlet opening.

For greatest safety it is important to use non-corrosive aquarium accessories such as gang valves. The type pictured here is constructed from non-metallic material. Courtesy of Penn-Plax Plastics, Inc.

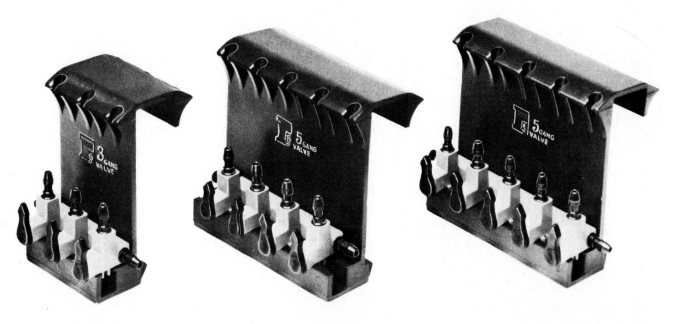

Gaterin orientalis

Myripristis murdjan

Chaetodon xanthurus

An array of marine tropical fish generally imported regularly from the Indo-Pacific. Photos by M. Goto.

Pomacanthus semicirculatus

Abudefduf melanopus

Dascyllus reticulatus

Chaetodon bennetti

Chaetodon trifasciatus

Example of a good type of undergravel filtration system. Courtesy Rolf C. Hagen Co.

general remove organic materials such as vitamins, colored materials in solution, or many other materials readily taken up by activated carbon. Probably, the resins are best avoided until we know more about their action in sea water.

BIOLOGICAL FILTERS

Biological filtration implies the use of bacteria or other living organisms to break down waste products. These will rapidly build up in almost any kind of filter but are usually discarded with clogged filter material by the time they are becoming really effective. Any filter bed has bacteria growing over the surface of its material, whether this is glass wool, fine sand, activated charcoal or almost anything else. Eventually, they are liable to form an impenetrable coating or nearly so, which interferes with the action of physico-chemically active materials. However, they take over some of the functions of such materials, but the drawback in a filter

which is not intended to be a biological filter is that the bacteria prevent the original activity from continuing but do not usually have a large enough surface area to settle on, to enable them to function fully instead. A biological filter needs to be extensive in the total area available for bacterial or other growth, usually algal growth. The very large surface area of clean finely divided activated charcoal does not finish up as an equivalent total area of bacteria, because the porous charcoal gets clogged by them.

The ideal biological filter is a sub-sand filter covering the whole of the base of the aquarium, with a sufficient depth of a suitable material such as coarse sand, gravel, crushed shells or coral of such a grade as to give an adequate flow of water over a very large total surface. Alternately, it is an external filter as large or larger than the tank itself, which may however be deep rather than shallow, as is the bottom layer of gravel, etc. Such filters are very popular in fresh-water and marine tanks already, but they have been used in marine tanks as though they are merely mechanical or mechanical plus chemical in action, according to their nature. It has therefore been the custom to advise cleaning of the filter bed at quite frequent intervals —varying from a few weeks to a few months— which may be the very time when its biological action has only just fully developed.

The details of the processes taking place in a biological filter will be discussed in later chapters, and it is sufficient to say here that when fully in action, this type of equipment breaks down waste products to harmless simple chemicals which will in part pass into the atmosphere, in part be discarded in water changes, absorbed by activated charcoal, or taken up by algae if these are allowed to grow in the tank. The filter bed should not be disturbed until it is so clogged that it ceases to perform its function, when it should be *partially* replaced or washed, leaving sufficient material still charged with bacteria to carry on the good work at an adequate level.

Changes in our views of the function and handling of sub-sand filters necessitate changes in design, if we are to be satisfied with the equipment. When an air-lift is used in sea water splash-back or creeping back into the air-tube occurs gradually and it becomes blocked with a stubborn deposit which does not readily redissolve. When it is the custom to take the equipment down at frequent intervals this may not matter, as it can often be dealt with before it is a nuisance. If, however, we intend to leave a sub-sand filter undisturbed for long periods, even years, this type of blockage can be a severe trouble as it cannot be corrected without delving under the gravel. For this reason, and also because it happens to be a more efficient system anyway, the air-tube should pass down the interior of a wide air-lift, preferably with a small airstone to give a well diffused mixture of bubbles and water to rise upwards. Removal

Skeleton of mushroom coral (*Fungia*). Living *Fungia* are quite hardy and attractive; they feed on fine dry foods and newly hatched brine shrimp. Photo by Dr. H.R. Axelrod.

Painted sweetlips, *Spilotichthys pictus*. The juvenile is more colorful than the adult (bottom). Photos by M. Goto.

Clown sweet-lips, *Gaterin chaetodonoides.* Adults may be too large for the average home tank. Juveniles (bottom) are more attractive and popular. Top photo by Dr. D. Terver, Nancy Aquarium, bottom photo by K.H. Choo.

of the air-tube for changing the air-stone or other diffuser used is then simple and can be done without disturbance to the filter.

The best material for a sub-sand filter is probably shellgrit (crushed shells) or crushed coral, because they contain calcium carbonate and can help to maintain pH and calcium levels. As bacterial coating occurs, the availability of the calcium carbonate falls, but never to zero. If other materials, such as river gravel or granite are used, adequate calcium carbonate sources should be maintained elsewhere, in the form of coral, shells, or another filter. The bed should be 2–4″ deep, with as fine a granule size as the slots in the filter allow. The correct choice of a medium which does not fall through under the filter and block it

is again the more important the longer we hope to leave the sub-sand filter undisturbed. A filter with slots wider than about 1/20″ is undesirable, as it will not hold back the inevitable proportion of fine particles present in even the best graded gravels of not too coarse a nature. The gravel should be nominally of about 1/10″–1/5″ in size, not more, or it will not offer a large enough total surface area and in addition it will allow passage to too much gross particulate debris and uneaten food. A little does not matter, but large amounts tend to foul the water and cannot be dealt with by the bacteria expeditiously. It is all a matter of maintaining a nice balance of the factors involved, upon which success so much depends.

Gravel composed of different-size particles is not desirable for use with an undergravel filter. Fine particles fall through the filter slots and block up the system. Photo by M.F. Roberts.

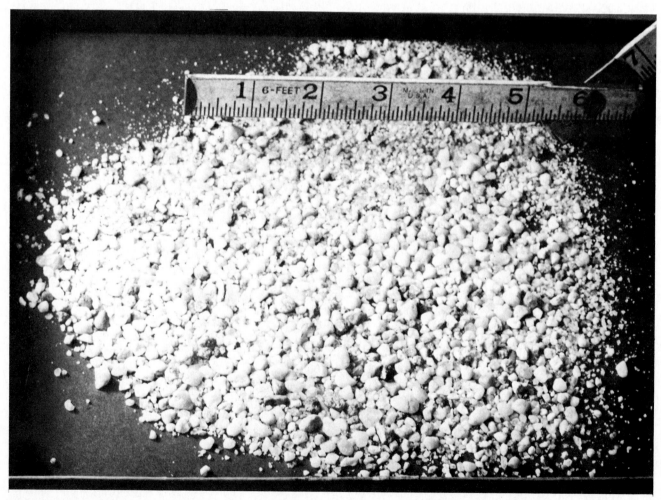

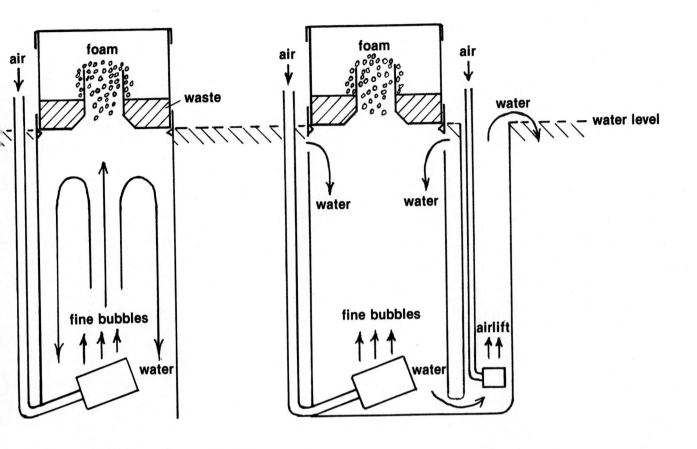

Two relatively simple air-stripping devices. That to the right employs a counter-current principle, with water flowing against the air-stream, and is the more suitable for simultaneous ozone treatment via the incoming air.

PROTEIN SKIMMING (Air-stripping)

A further physico-chemical method which is not really filtration uses foam fractionation, long used in sewage treatment but only recently adapted on a micro scale for aquarium use. Some of us were very skeptical about such methods in the aquarium, particularly because the early advocates for their use misunderstood the principles involved and presented very unlikely sounding arguments in their favor. Thus, they were first asserted to remove fish urine from the water, perhaps because the liquids they produced were often yellow in appearance.

The principles are in fact as follows. When a mass of fine bubbles is passed through polluted water it causes foaming and frothing to occur. The greater the pollution, particularly if by proteinaceous matter, the greater the foaming. If this foam is "skimmed" off by suitable equip-

ment it carries with it much of the pollutants, again in particular the so-called surface active materials which form a film on the surface of bubbles and are carried up into the foam. The equipment is therefore to some extent self-adjusting, and if it is used with pure sea water little foaming occurs and not much is collected. As the water collects waste products, these will help to cause greater foaming, which they will accompany in part into the skimmed off portion and eventually be discarded. Really loaded water produces a copious dark brown foam which may need removing once or twice daily.

Protein skimmers vary in design from simple tubes with an air-stone at the base, to fairly complicated counter-current equipment in which a flow of aquarium water is forced in a downward direction against the up-flowing stream of air. They remove some, but not all

Emperor angelfish, *Pomacanthus imperator*, one of the most colorful reef fishes. Adults of this widely distributed species grow up to a foot in length. Photo by M. Goto.

Juvenile emperor angelfish, showing a color pattern strikingly distinct from that of the adult. The circular pattern near the tail is characteristic for the species. Photo by M. Goto.

Filter units that use diatomaceous earth as the filter medium provide extreme clarity to the water. Courtesy Vortex Innerspace Products.

of the material that activated charcoal removes, and it is not usually necessary to use both. However, activated charcoal may also have other functions discussed when considering biological filters, and if a choice has to be made, it is probably the best of the physico-chemical group when intelligently used.

OZONE

Ozone, or O_3, is a very active form of oxygen gas which is unstable and readily gives off atomic oxygen, O, and a molecule of normal oxygen gas, O_2. The extra atom of oxygen combines with any substance not already saturated with oxygen and usually renders it less active chemically than it was to begin with. As an example, nitrites, such as sodium nitrite, $NaNO_2$, are highly poisonous in the aquarium, and are formed in the course of bacterial attack on waste products. A high nitrite level will kill all fishes, but in the presence of ozone, nitrites cannot survive, and will be oxidized to nitrates (e.g. sodium nitrate, $NaNO_3$). These are hardly toxic at all, and can be tolerated at 100 times or more the concentration of nitrites, and so the action of ozone is highly beneficial as far as nitrites are concerned.

This situation extends to many other compounds, and to the effects of ozone on bacteria, viruses and many other parasites, which are killed by the gas. So are fishes if it is present in excess, and so ozone must either be metered with care into the aquarium, or it must react with the water apart from the aquarium direct, in a filter system, or in a protein skimmer, for example. Ozone is introduced into the air supply to the aquarium by passing it through an ozoniser, a high tension electric discharge tube which releases a measured amount of ozone per hour into the aeration system. If it is released directly into the tank, a somewhat hazardous procedure if effective dosage is to be achieved, about 0.2 to 0.3 mg per gallon per hour is advised, or temporarily for short periods up to 0.4 mg per gallon per hour. More will cause distress to the fishes and destruction of their protective mucus and even skin.

It is much safer to ozonise into a skimmer, when excess ozone will pass into the air before the water gets back into the tank, or in a filter, when the same occurs. If heavy ozonisation plus safety is required, the water can be passed through activated charcoal before it is returned to the aquarium. The advantage of direct ozonisation in the tank is that it gets everywhere and destroys bacteria, including unfortunately those in a biological filter if such is in use. The other disadvantage has already been mentioned. If a biological filter is used, which will most often be so, minimal ozone treatment is mandatory unless via a skimmer or filter or suchlike.

Ozone has been found to be particularly helpful in the invertebrate or mixed tank. Its effects are sometimes dramatic, presumably

Clownfish appear to be protected from anemone stings by (1) mucus (the fish is killed if the mucus is washed off), (2) immune reaction which can be specific to a given anemone species. Photo by G. Budich.

A box crab
(*Calappa*). Box
crabs can use
their powerful
claws to
extricate live
snails out of
their protective
shells. Photo by
D. Faulkner.

Many shore crabs are of world-wide distribution and are easy to collect. Some of these crabs are able to survive with only limited access to water for moistening gills. Bottom photo shows the underside of a female crab. Photos by Dr. S. Frank.

Top: feather duster worm (*Sabellastarte indica*). Bottom: serpulid worm (*Spirographis* sp.). These tube worms catch plankton with their tentacles equipped with fine hair-like processes. They can be fed with very finely chopped clams, almost liquid in consistency. Top photo by Dr. D. Terver, bottom photo by Dr. H.R. Axelrod.

because many invertebrates are highly sensitive to toxins at levels which do not affect most fishes. In a tank of about 250 gallons capacity containing corals, anemones, sea squirts, scallops, cowries, small squid and many other invertebrates, a breakdown of the ozonising equipment was followed within a few hours by alarming collapse of many of the inhabitants, restored to health within a similar period when the equipment was repaired. This tank was perhaps overstocked, in the sense that no tank should be so crowded that such rapid changes could occur, but it certainly provided an example of what ozonisers can do. The particular advantage in the invertebrate tank is that biological or fine filtration may not be in use, because it tends to remove the plankton and to starve organisms like corals and filter feeders such as bivalve moluscs and sea squirts.

The danger to a biological filter is thus not important, and the full advantage of ozone can be realized.

Relatively cheap ozonisers are set at fixed rate of discharge, such as 10 mg per hour, and must be suited to the size of tank, or tanks, they serve. More useful but more expensive equipment offers a range of 3–25 mg or 5–50 mg per hour, and is clearly much better to use. The ozonising tube is sensitive to moisture and for long life must be protected from it. Use a dehumidifier, such as a tube of moisture absorbing crystals, or even anhydrous calcium chloride to absorb the moisture before the air passes into the ozoniser. Either is inexpensive, can be regenerated by heat, and is a wise investment to protect the much more expensive ozone reactor.

A gorgonian with extended polyps. Photo by R. Straughan.

Ultra-violet sterilizers come in a number of different makes and models and can be used with either marine tanks or freshwater tanks. Courtesy Nektonics and Hawaiian Marine Imports.

ULTRAVIOLET LIGHT

Sterilization by ultraviolet (UV) irradiation is a common practice commercially, and suitable equipment is sold for aquarium use. Oddly enough, its real value in the home aquarium seems not to have been very well established, and it is probably the least frequently used method. It cannot be introduced directly in effective dosage in the aquarium itself, as it would harm the fishes, causing blindness among other things. Instead, the water is passed over UV tubes so that a fairly thin layer is irradiated at a time, and returned in a sterile or partially sterilized state to the tank. These tubes are best shielded by plastic covers so that the UV rays do not harm the observer, as they can also affect ourselves in high dosage.

A flow of 10 gallons per minute over two 33″ slimline UV tubes in series, with a water layer of $\frac{1}{8}$″ surrounding the tubes, is said to be adequate to sterilize completely, and has been demonstrated to aid in bivalve mollusk culture.

However, this system was applied to a constant intake of new water, not to recirculation from the same tank. The drawback, also applicable to any recirculation system of treatment is that when water is taken from the tank, not all of it is forced to circulate through the external equipment and some dead spots may persist indefinitely. An additional hazard is that bacteria or parasites remain on surfaces within the tank, so that no pretense of sterility in the tank as a whole can be maintained.

UV light is used in some public aquaria to cause fluorescence in corals, many of which show beautiful and different fluorescent colors under its influence. It is of interest that to stimulate this fluorescence, the UV light has to pass through several feet of water, and the common belief that it is absorbed by a few inches or less of water thickness is clearly untrue, at least for the wave lengths concerned with fluorescence.

A cowrie (*Cypraea*). This is a living specimen photographed as it crawled on the aquarium wall. Cowries can emit a substance toxic to other animals. Photo by R. Steene.

Feather stars (Crinoidea). Feather stars are very colorful but unfortunately also fragile animals. Arms fall off by autotomy (self mutilation). Photo by Dr. H.R. Axelrod.

The cuttlefish, *Sepia officinalis*, presents very few problems to its keeper. However, all cephalopods need a well-aerated and large tank. Photo by H. Hansen.

The sea cucumber *Paracucumaria tricolor*, found in deeper water off the coast of Australia. This species' bright coloration is not typical of sea cucumbers, which are often plain-looking, brown or black in color. Photo by R. Steene.

Chapter 2

The Water

NATURAL SEA-WATER

The water in the sea is a very complex solution which defies complete analysis. Not only does it contain dissolved salts and organic compounds, including enzymes, vitamins and other relatively high molecular weight compounds, but in its natural state it is often loaded with plankton, debris and bacteria. As soon as it is collected it starts to change, so that the water in an aquarium, large or small, is never quite the same as that in the ocean, and is often very different from it. The changes are much greater than those undergone by fresh-water, which doesn't, with its much smaller load of dissolved materials, offer the same scope for complications.

The salt content of natural sea-water is usually between 3.3% and 3.8%, as long as it is collected away from estuaries and such. The main constituents are the metals sodium, magnesium, calcium, potassium and strontium, in combination with chloride, sulphate, carbonate, bicarbonate, bromide and borate ions. The minor inorganic constituents include almost every other chemical element, constituting the trace elements, some of which are of importance to life. It is impossible, by the way, to say that sea water contains so much sodium chloride ($NaCl$), so much potassium chloride (KCl), so much sodium sulphate (Na_2SO_4) and so forth because all these substances are dissolved, partly ionized (i.e. broken into positive metallic ions, Na^+, K^+, Ca^{++}, etc. and nega-tive non-metallic ions, Cl^-, SO_4^{--}, etc.) and partly combined at any one moment. That is why different formulae for making up artificial sea water may seem to be contradictory. They often differ quite a bit in total content of different elements, but even those which aim at copying natural sea water may do so by different salt combinations.

The major constituents outlined above account for over 99% of the weight of dissolved material in sea water. Such water, at a specific gravity (see below) of 1.025 at 60°F (15°C), has the following overall composition in grams per liter. These figures differ a little, but not significantly as far as life is concerned, according to methods of analysis and the samples taken, etc.

Metals:

Sodium (Na)	10.77 g
Magnesium (Mg)	1.30 g
Calcium (Ca)	0.41 g
Potassium (K)	0.39 g
Strontium (Sr)	0.01 g

Bases:

Chloride (Cl)	19.37 g
Sulphate (SO_4)	2.71 g
Bromide (Br)	0.07 g
Boric acid (H_3BO_3)	0.026 g
Carbonates, bicarbonates and free CO_2	0.025 g approx.

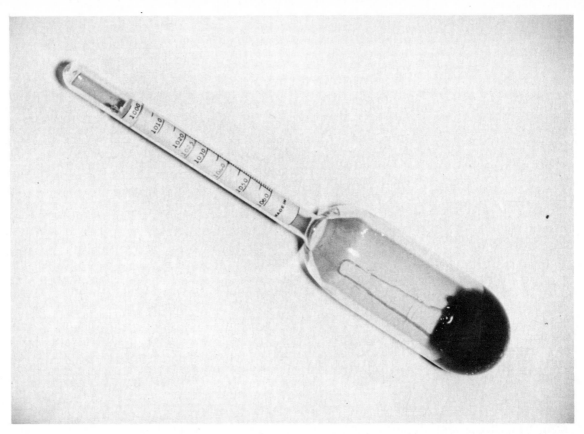

Hydrometer. An inexpensive but very useful piece of equipment. Photo by M.F. Roberts.

Other:

Organic matter		0.001–0.0025 g
Oxygen gas (O_2)		0.008 g
Nitrogen gas (N_2)		0.013 g
All the rest		0.005 g

A rather crude artificial sea water (from Lyman and Fleming, 1940, J. Marine Res. **3**, 134) can thus be made from the elements, etc., at the top of the table, combined together as suitable salts such as:

Sodium chloride	(NaCl)	23.48 g
Magnesium chloride	($MgCl_2 \cdot 6H_2O$)	4.98 g
Sodium sulphate	($Na_2SO_4 \cdot 10H_2O$)	3.92 g
Calcium chloride	($CaCl_2$)	1.10 g
Potassium chloride	(KCl)	0.664 g
Sodium bicarbonate	($NaHCO_3$)	0.192 g
Potassium bromide	(KBr)	0.096 g
Boric acid	(H_3BO_3)	0.026 g
Strontium chloride	($SrCl_2$)	0.024 g
		per liter of H_2O

This topic will, however, be taken up in greater detail later on.

The minor constituents in sea-water vary much more in different localities than do the major ones. In addition, analyses by different methods and according to different authors are sometimes very discrepant. However, ranges for what seem to be the most biologically important of these but not necessarily the most abundant, are approximately as follows in micrograms (μg) per liter:

Metals:

Aluminium (Al)	0–1900μg!
Barium (Ba)	30– 90μg
Copper (Cu)	1– 25μg
Iron (Fe)	up to 60μg
Lithium (Li)	100μg
Manganese (Mn)	1– 10μg
Molybdenum (Mo)	0.3–16μg
Rubidium (Rb)	200μg
Vanadium (Va)	0.2–7.0μg
Zinc (Zn)	14μg

Non-metals:

Phosphate (PO_4)	0–60μg
Silicon (Si)	0–3μg
Fluorine (F)	1400μg
Iodine (I)	50μg

Slipper lobster (*Scyllarides*). This omnivorous crustacean digs and burrows in the sand. Photo by M. Goto.

The bumble bee shrimp, *Gnathophyllum americanus*, is reported to feed on sea urchin tube feet. Photo by D.L. Savitt and R.B. Silver.

This marine shrimp, *Enoplometopus occidentalis*, was taken from deep water (100 feet) in Oahu, Hawaii. Photo by Dr. J.E. Randall.

Red-spotted shrimp (*Hymenocerus*). Claws are missing in this specimen. *Hymenocerus* subsists on sea stars in the wild but also eats coral and anemones and is a danger if kept with them. Photo by A. Norman.

It is abundantly clear that a great deal more needs to be done in determining the composition of sea-water samples and the significance of many of the substances it contains. Those listed above appear from various trials, and from knowledge of the needs of various living organisms, to be the elements necessary for life, particularly plant and invertebrate life. Some of the analyses do not seem to have been repeated since the 1930's and 40's and are clearly in need of reassessment with modern techniques.

SOME RELEVANT MEASUREMENTS

Specific gravity has been mentioned above, and is the measure of total dissolved salts most frequently quoted in the aquarium literature. It relates the density of salt water to that of pure fresh water, and is normally thought of as being 1.025 at 60°F (approx. 15°C). The exact measurement yielded by a particular sample of water depends on the temperature and for scientific purposes the rather unwieldy temperature of 4°C (approx. 40°F) is used as a

Relationships between specific gravity and salinity (percentage of salts) at different temperatures.

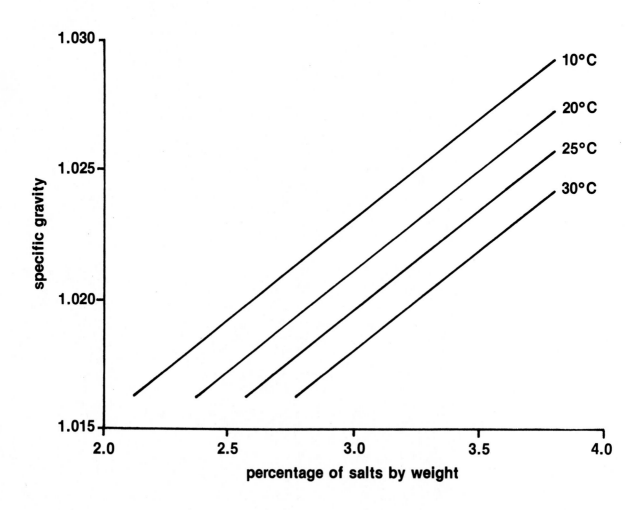

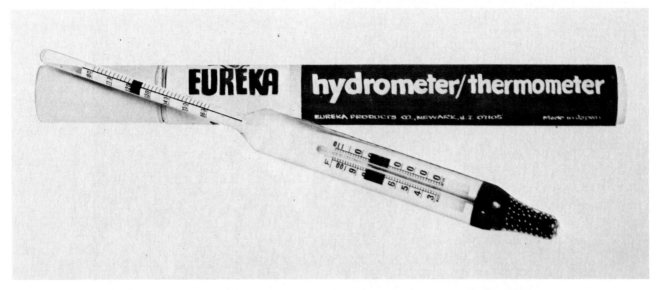

Hydrometer and thermometer combined in one instrument. Courtesy of Eureka Products Co.

standard. The specific gravity is then defined as the ratio of its weight to that of an equal volume of distilled water.

Specific gravity is measured with a hydrometer, an instrument which floats in the water and has a loaded base and graduations on a projecting stem covering a range suitable for any particular purpose. Those for aquarium use normally cover the range 1.000 to 1.050—i.e. from fresh water to a brine twice the density of sea-water. These aquarium hydrometers are usually calibrated for 60°F, as quoted above, and conversion tables are available for other temperatures. Roughly, a rise or fall of 10°F around 60°F is accompanied by a fall or rise of 0.001 in specific gravity. Thus, a reading of 1.023 at 80°F (27°C) is equivalent to 1.025 at 60°F. The tropical tank will therefore be kept at around 1.023, rather than 1.025.

Salinity is closely related to specific gravity, and describes the percentage of total salts by weight, dissolved in the water. By definition, salinity is not dependent on temperature, or hardly so, although the exact measurement of it may be. There is a series of relationships between salinity and specific gravity for each temperature. A specific gravity of 1.025 corresponds approximately to a salinity of 3.1% at

freezing point (32°F, 0°C), of 3.25% at 10°C (50°F), 3.5% at 20°C (68°F) and 3.7% at 30°C (86°F). These relationships are of importance when synthetic sea water is being made up—usually, we take 3.5% as being about right. Fine adjustments, if needed, can most easily be made with the help of a hydrometer in the final mix.

Hydrogen ion concentration is measured on the pH scale, and tells us about the relative acidity or alkalinity of fluids. A pH of 7.0 is neutral, of less than 7.0 acid, and above it alkaline. In contrast to fresh-water, which varies in nature from perhaps as low as pH 4.0 to as high as pH 8.0 or even 9.0, sea-water in its natural state is always alkaline, around pH 8.2, with quite narrow limits at the surface of the open ocean of 8.0 to 8.3. At great depths, or when polluted, it may fall to 7.6 (extreme value quoted), but this would be quite exceptional. In the aquarium, such a fall is common, and has to be kept in mind.

The greatest natural influence on pH is carbon dioxide; when sea water is in equilibrium with fresh air, the pH is as quoted above. As CO_2 accumulates, the pH falls, this effect covering a range down to about 7.4 in all normal circumstances. Salinity and tempera-

The harlequin tuskfish, *Lienardella fasciata*, is death on other smaller fishes but it is a beauty. Photo by M. Goto.

The longnosed filefish, *Oxymonacanthus longirostris,* is a prized aquarium fish but hard to keep. Photo by M. Goto.

Centropyge vroliki, the pearly-scaled angelfish, is more manageable than its larger relatives. Its diet should be supplemented with vegetable matter. Photo by M. Goto.

The longnosed butterflyfish, *Forcipiger flavissimus*, is a very good aquarium fish. Photo by K.H. Choo.

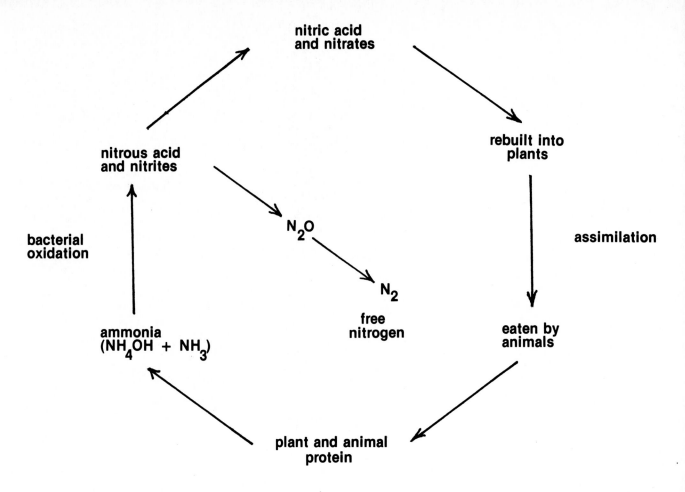

The nitrogen cycle.

ture have minor effects on pH, but nothing of importance. A further set of important influences in the aquarium is the accumulation of waste elements, products of bacterial decomposition, crowding of fishes and various other types of mismanagement which may cause falls to dangerous levels.

Dissolved gases are rather difficult to measure, except indirectly via pH in the case of CO_2, but the oxygen (O_2) concentration is the main thing to know about. In fact, except in large public aquaria, O_2 concentration is very rarely actually measured, but its level must be constantly borne in mind as a most important factor, more important than in the fresh-water tank. Oxygen is less soluble in sea-water than in fresh-water, yet most salt-water fishes are more sensitive to lack of it. The percentage saturation with oxygen must be kept higher than in the fresh-water tank, and this is achieved by adequate maintenance techniques. These include purity of water, brisk aeration and surface movement, not too high a tem-

perature in relation to normal for the specimens being kept, and avoidance of overcrowding.

At the surface of cold oceans, the O_2 content may be as high as 7 ml per liter (nearly saturated), but it falls to as little as 4 ml/liter in the tropics. There are areas near to the surface in tropical seas where the O_2 content is very low, usually because of "blooms" of oxygen-consuming organisms, resulting in perhaps as low as 0.5 or 1.0 ml per liter, which is only 10 or 20% saturation or less. This could not sustain fishes for very long, although plankton may survive.

The nitrogen cycle is one of several metabolic cycles going on in natural and captive waters, and the most important for the aquarist, as far as measurement is concerned. We shall see later the importance of measurements of ammonia (NH_4), nitrite (NO_2) and nitrate (NO_3) in tank water. These would all have very low values in water from the open seas, but they may accumulate in tank water and

62

particularly the first two may readily reach toxic levels. Methods for their measurement are not very satisfactory in the hands of amateurs, but if we do the best we can with the available equipment it is better than nothing. These methods usually depend on color changes, as do pH measurements in the commonly available kits, and the changes in hue or intensity, or both, are sometimes hard to interpret very accurately. The best techniques are those that provide the aquarist with a comparator—a set of tubes of colored liquids or a set of colored glasses—with which to compare his own preparation from the water he is testing. Even with pH, do not depend on comparisons with colored prints or charts, and do not use papers which are dipped into the water and change color according to its condition. Such papers are often grossly misleading in the results they give and tend to deteriorate on keeping.

COLLECTING SEA-WATER

Very many marine aquarium keepers must depend on dealers for their samples of sea-water or a substitute. Those lucky enough to be able to collect and transport their own may be glad of some hints.

Only collect water from unpolluted areas; even if it looks clean and wholesome it may contain insecticides, chemical residues, and a host of toxic substances if gathered from inshore or estuarine areas, or even near to agricultural areas adjacent to the open coast. This makes for problems, but increasing degrees of pollution are the facts of life nowadays and have to be faced. It is safer to use a good artificial mix than to risk poisoning your fishes with impure natural water. Unfortunately it is not feasible to try to test for all the varieties of pollutant that may be present.

Changes in nitrogen-containing compounds which occur in a newly set-up tank.

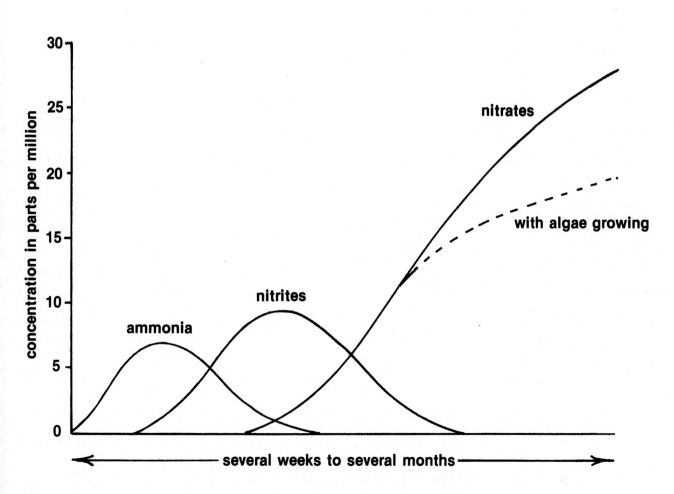

Pterois antennata, the spot-fin lionfish, is just as poisonous as the related lionfish *Pterois volitans.* Photo by M. Goto.

Blue devil, *Abudefduf cyanea.* Inexpensive and easy to keep, but the blue color fades with passage of time. Photo by M. Goto.

A well-planted marine tank like this one requires very intensive light for maintenance. Except under close supervision, this tank would be a smelly mess in a short time. Photo by Dr. D. Terver.

One-spot butterfly-fish, *Chaetodon unimaculatus*. This species is difficult to collect and therefore seldom sold in pet shops.

Lizardfishes (*Synodus*), ferocious in appearance as well as appetite. Not to be included with other fishes. Photos by M. Goto.

Water from a mangrove swamp is generally not safe for keeping fish. The water is brackish and may contain harmful organic substances. Photo by Dr. H.R. Axelrod.

When you have found a spot which experience (yours or others') has shown to be safe, store your collected water in a set of as large vessels as possible, in the dark, and in glass, *safe* plastic or vessels lined with large plastic bags or sheets, if there is any doubt about safety. If the water can be used immediately, as in filling a new tank, or very shortly after storage, within at most a day, this is fairly safe, but risk of disease is always present. If it cannot be used within a day, keep it for at least 2–3 weeks, since stored water rapidly undergoes changes, some irreversible, of which the most prominent is increase in bacterial content. The smaller the vessel in which it is stored, the greater the increase in bacterial count. This appears to be related to the area of the inner surface of the vessel in relation to the volume it contains, as bacterial proliferation mostly occurs there. This bacterial bloom occurs typically with a maximum at between 2 days and 10 days after collection, more dependent on temperature

than anything else if other factors such as nutrients are equal. After a few weeks storage, the bacterial count dies down, but rarely returns to as low as it was initially. In vessels of only a few gallons capacity, the rise is from a few hundred or less per ml to perhaps half a million; in larger storage tanks it is lower, but still spectacular. This rise may be accompanied by severe oxygen depletion.

Another change occurring on storage is the death of plankton (animal and vegetable) which will tend to prolong bacterial growth since it provides nourishment for them. After several weeks, a sediment will settle out on the bottom of the storage vessels, quite often a remarkably big one. This consists of dead plankton, bacteria and other debris. Avoid resuspending it. Small changes in pH and nitrogenous compound content of the stored water may occur, but these appear to be surprisingly small in view of the events which are happening. Ammonia and nitrite levels, for instance, do not usually increase. However, in mildly polluted water containing organic residues, ammonia and nitrite levels can rise to toxic proportions and may be dangerous for up to 3 months, when they gradually decline. This is a further reason for avoiding even mildly polluted water.

Usually, water siphoned off from storage vessels after standing for 3 weeks or longer is safe, and after temperature adjustment can be used in the aquarium. Even fine filtration prior to storage makes little difference to this rule, but would make the minimum period (say 2 weeks) safer than it would be otherwise.

SYNTHETIC SALT-WATER

A great advance in marine fish keeping has followed the availability of satisfactory synthetic mixes. Evaporated sea-salt comes out in layers of different chemical constitution and is hard to mix back in proper proportions. In addition, it does not reconstitute as the original

article because of chemical changes which occur. It is thus safer to use a good synthetic mix. Few claim that any such mix is as good as pure sea-water, but it is likely to be better than polluted water, and may, in any case, be all that can be obtained in sufficient quantities without vast cost. A few of the quite complex mixes used in public aquaria, or available now in the smaller quantities needed by aquarists, are very good indeed and can support most invertebrates. They are fairly expensive and last no better in the aquarium than sea-water does, and so need periodic replacement.

The Cleveland modification of a formula evolved in the Frankfurt Aquarium is an example of an advanced synthetic water, made up in stages to avoid precipitation of poorly soluble constituents, and to help to ensure proper quantities of trace elements, which tend to get inadequately mixed if included in large batches. Here are the quantities needed to make up 100 U.S. gallons of specific gravity 1.025:

Natural sea water is safe to use only after storage. Even apparently safe water in a reef area like this should not be used immediately. Photo by Dr. H.R. Axelrod.

Moorish idols,
Zanclus canescens,
are very difficult to
keep for any length of
time; they sometimes
die off for no obvious
reason. Photo by
M. Goto.

The golden-headed sleeper, *Eleotriodes strigata,* requires a sandy bottom for burrowing
and small crustaceans for food. Photo by M. Goto.

Shrimpfish (*Aeoliscus strigatus*). This fish swims inside the spaces among the spines of long-spined sea urchins and keeps pace as the sea urchin perambulates. Photo by P. Laboute.

Directions for Use

Part I

NaCl	10.5	kg
$MgSO_4 \cdot 7H_2O$	2.62	kg
$MgCl \cdot 6H_2O$	2.04	kg
KCl	0.274	kg
$NaHCO_3$	0.079	kg
$SrCl_2 \cdot 6H_2O$	7.5	g
$MnSO_4 \cdot H_2O$	1.5	g
$Na_2HPO_4 \cdot 7H_2O$	1.25	g
LiCl	0.375	g
$Na_2MoO_4 \cdot 2H_2O$	0.375	g

Dissolve in warm water and keep fairly concentrated. Then add Part II and bring to specific gravity 1.025—around 100 gallons (US).

Part II

$CaCl_2$	0.52	kg

Dissolve in hot water and add to Part I.

Directions for Use

Part III

KBr	270	g
Ca gluconate	6.25	g
KI	0.90	g

Dissolve in 2 liters of distilled water and add 80 ml per 100 gallons of Parts I plus II.

Part IV

$Al(SO_4)_3$	4.5	g
$CuSO_4 \cdot 5H_2O$	4.3	g
RbCl	1.5	g
$ZnSO_4 \cdot 7H_2O$	0.96	g
$CoSO_4$	0.50	g

Dissolve in 2 liters of distilled water and add 80 ml per 100 gallons of Parts I plus II after Part III has been added.

Excellent preparations of artificial marine salts are available commercially. They are packaged in different weights for convenience. See text for additional comments.   Courtesy of Aquarium Systems, Inc., Jungle Laboratories, and Hawaiian Marine Imports.

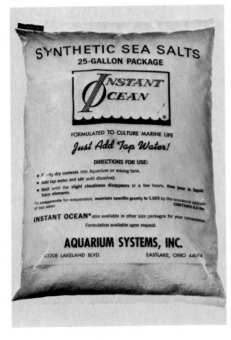

A cleaner wrasse (*Labroides dimidiatus*) cleaning its tank-mate, a Hawaiian surgeonfish   (*Acanthurus triostegus*). Photo by M. Kocar.

If only a few hundred gallons are to be made up, proportionately less of Parts III and IV can be made up by a professional chemist, using smaller quantities weighed on a reasonably accurate balance.

The final solution should be aerated for 24–48 hours, to equilibrate it with the atmosphere and to stabilize the pH, which should be about 8.3. It is quite in order to make a brine containing up to 3 times the above concentrations and to dilute it in the aquarium itself if more convenient. This can save unnecessary carting of buckets of mix at 1.025.

The composition of salt mixes available commercially is not usually revealed. Analysis has shown that some are very simple and not likely to be very satisfactory. The best are likely to defy any ordinary attempt at complete analysis, because the equipment necessary to detect and measure everything present will rarely be available within a single laboratory, remembering that the minute traces of some substances are hard to estimate even with the best of modern equipment. An exception to the secrecy rule is *Instant Ocean* (Aquarium Systems Inc., East Lake, Ohio), the complete formula and ionic composition of which is quoted by Spotte in "Fish and Invertebrate Culture" (Wiley-Interscience, 1970).

The black-backed butterflyfish, *Chaetodon melannotus*, is one of the best to keep, quite hardy and eats well. Photo by M. Goto.

Pseudochromis paccagnellae looks beautiful and harmless but actually is a voracious and pugnacious fish. Photo by Dr. H.R. Axelrod.

The unicorn leather-jacket, *Alutera monoceros*. This member of the filefish family (Monacanthidae) eats a variety of invertebrates like sponges, corals, worms, mollusks and crustaceans. Photo by M. Goto.

Bolbometapon bicolor, the two-colored parrotfish, undergoes several color changes before reaching the adult coloration distinct from the juvenile coloration seen here. Photo by K.H. Choo.

Sea horse (*Hippocampus*). The sea horse to the right, a male, is "pregnant." A female deposited fertilized eggs into the male's pouch earlier. After incubation the young are "born." Photo by R. Straughan.

Some interesting comparisons have been made between synthetic mixes and sea-water. These are somewhat difficult to interpret, because of the big differences that exist between systems and management of them, but what emerges seems to be that under good management, with no overcrowding and with adequate replacement of part of the water from time to time, there is little difference as far as fishes are concerned, particularly with complex mixes. The simple mixes do not support even vertebrates beyond a few months unless some natural sea-water is added. Only the best mixes support most invertebrates indefinitely, and again only under very good management. One account gives details of what happened when the author purposely overcrowded and stressed his tanks, in one of the few really meaningful tests with many simultaneous tanks. The results were spectacular. Every tank containing synthetic salt water went bad quite rapidly but no tank with the natural article did so at this early period! The author's own experience is similar.

CHANGES WITHIN THE AQUARIUM
Nitrogenous matter

The nitrogen cycle has been mentioned when discussing measurements of water quality. It now needs fuller discussion. It is a cycle by which organic nitrogen-containing matter (i.e. proteins mainly) is broken down by various routes which include digestion by fishes, decay of uneaten food and of aquarium debris, and decay of voided fecal matter to ammonia, thence via the action of bacteria such as *Nitrosomonas* to nitrites, and by the action of other bacteria such as *Nitrobacter* to nitrates, assimilation by algae and other bacteria back

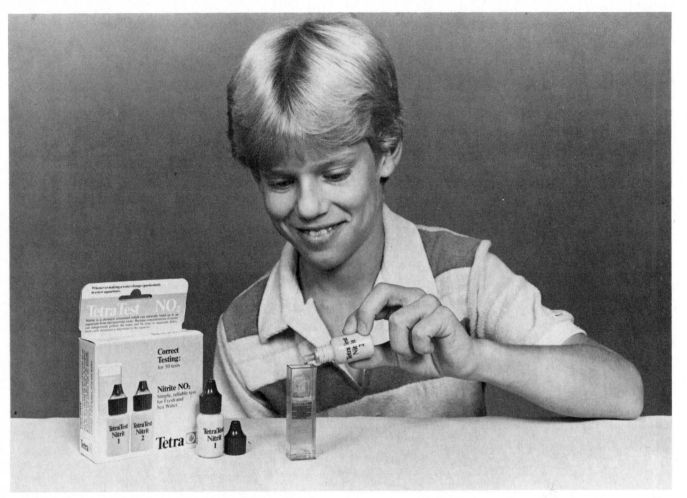

The nitrite/nitrate cycle in marine aquariums is of great importance; kits that monitor nitrite levels are easily obtainable and relatively inexpensive. Courtesy Tetra Sales.

into organic matter or further reduction (via nitrites again or other routes) to nitrogen gas, which escapes from the aquarium. Ammonia and nitrites are highly toxic, and it is this part of the cycle that causes trouble in the aquarium.

If a salt water aquarium has no filter, ammonia and nitrites will build up rapidly unless frequent changes of water are made, and/or there are very few fishes present. This is why some form of filtration is necessary. If it has a frequently-changed filter bed, and thus is filtered only by mechanical and chemical means, removal of ammonia and nitrite depends on adequate uptake of these compounds by activated charcoal or the like (and there is no good substitute for charcoal in a filter) or oxidation by ozone. A degree of biological, i.e. bacterial, activity may be shown by accumulations of mulm, and by some build-up in whatever filters are used, but adequate biological filtration needs time to become established and

depends on ageing of the filter bed. So an aquarium can be maintained successfully by two basic systems:
(1) "Sterile" mechanical and chemical filtration or ozonization.
(2) Biological filtration utilizing bacterial and other actions.

The two can be combined in various ways to give the best of both worlds, but by one means or another, ammonia and nitrite levels must be kept down almost to zero. The maximum tolerable level of ammonia, for most fishes, is usually quoted as about 0.1 ppm (parts per million, or mg per liter) and of nitrites as about 0.25 ppm. However, even lower levels than these affect fishes in the long-term and many invertebrates short-term, so it is best to aim for virtually zero as far as measurements can go. Nitrates are much better tolerated, even though they remain low in the open ocean, and up to about 40 ppm seems safe in most circumstances.

Rhinomuraena ambonensis, one of the ribbon eels, should be kept in covered tanks only; it escapes through cracks between the lid and the tank. Photo by M. Goto.

The juvenile color pattern of this clown labrid, *Coris aygula*, will change with growth. Photo by R. Allard.

The sabre-toothed blenny, *Plagiotremus tapeinosoma*, hides in almost any type of opening in the reef including empty bottles, beer cans, etc. Photo by Dr. G.R. Allen.

Carbon dioxide

At the surface of the sea, the CO_2 in the air and it and its salts in the water are in equilibrium. CO_2 gas passes rather gradually through the air-water interface, and the turbulence normally associated with the ocean surface assists this passage. This is one reason why good stirring and surface movement is important in aquaria. There is an equilibrium which settles down under constant conditions with fixed proportions of the following compounds of ions:

$$CO_2 \rightleftharpoons CO_2 + H_2O \rightleftharpoons H_2CO_3$$
in air   in water   carbonic acid
$$\rightleftharpoons H^+ + HCO_3^- \rightleftharpoons H^+ + CO_3^{--}$$
ionization (1)   ionization (2)

The last four reactions occur in water. Borates in the water also take part in this system, but for simplicity are not separately shown. Carbonic and boric acids are the only weak acids of note in natural sea water, but not necessarily in the aquarium.

Changes in pH accompany changes in equilibrium in the above system. A low pH results from conditions in which little or no ionization (2) is occurring; thus at pH 7.5 in a tropical tank there will be about 3% of $CO_2 + H_2O$ or H_2CO_3, about 94% of H^+ (hydrogen ions) + HCO_3^- (bicarbonate ions), and 3% of $H^+ + CO_3^{--}$ (carbonate ions). At pH 8.3 (normal pH) there will be about 0.4% of $CO_2 + H_2O$ or H_2CO_3, about 83% of $H^+ + HCO_3^-$ ions, and 17% of $H^+ + CO_3^{--}$ ions. It takes shifts to extremes to cause pH changes beyond these limits. Such a system is the main *buffering* system within the sea or the tank, and it is on its stability that the pH of the aquarium mostly depends, as long as gross pollution is not allowed to occur. The fact that much of the carbonic acid in sea water will really be in the form of metallic salts—e.g. Na_2CO_3, etc., does not affect the situation, which is shown in terms of pure carbonic acid for ease of illustration.

Fiddler crab (*Uca*). Male specimen showing enlarged claw. Photo by F.A. Werner.

As well as the air-water interface exchange, of minor normal importance in the sea, but of major importance in the aquarium, there is production of CO_2 by animal (and plant) respiration and metabolism. In both situations, particularly near to the coast, there is also a carbonate source available in mineral carbonates contained in shells, shell-grit, corals and other carbonate deposits. In the fish tank, the presence of adequate mineral reserves may be critical, hence the great desirability of the presence of corals and carbonaceous rocks or gravel. The main carbonates concerned are calcium carbonate, $CaCO_3$, and magnesium carbonate $MgCO_3$.

Phosphorus

There is a phosphorus cycle in sea water, mainly concerned with the release of phosphates from decomposing matter and its subsequent uptake by bacteria, algae and animals and re-release. In the aquarium, as occasionally in nature, excess of phosphates can contribute to algae and other "blooms," when the water may become grossly cloudy because of an overfertilization and growth of one-celled organisms. Details of this cycle do not matter as phosphates are not harmful in moderate quantities and are a normal part of sea water, but they are part of the nutrition, particularly of plants, and should not be present in vast excess. An algal or bacterial bloom is unsightly and may be dangerous when the organisms exhaust some component of their food supply, die, and if not adequately dealt with by the filters, further pollute the water and deplete it of oxygen.

The hermit crab *Pagurus bernhardus*; without its protective mollusk shell, this crab is not expected to survive long in the wild. Photo by G. Marcuse.

Sabre-toothed blenny
(*Plagiotremus
tapeinosoma*). Rarely
seen in full view.
Photo by M. Goto.

The zebra blenny, *Meiacanthus grammistes*, is not as prone to hiding as other blennies. Accepts both live and pre-pared foods. Photo by K.H. Choo.

Hemitaurichthys polylepis

Chaetodon citrinellus

Odonus niger

Geniacanthus lamarcki

Except for the black triggerfish, *Odonus niger*, all the fishes shown here are difficult to keep. They may initially accept live brine shrimp and other foods, but they soon refuse to eat and subsequently starve to death or become easy prey to disease. Photos by M. Goto.

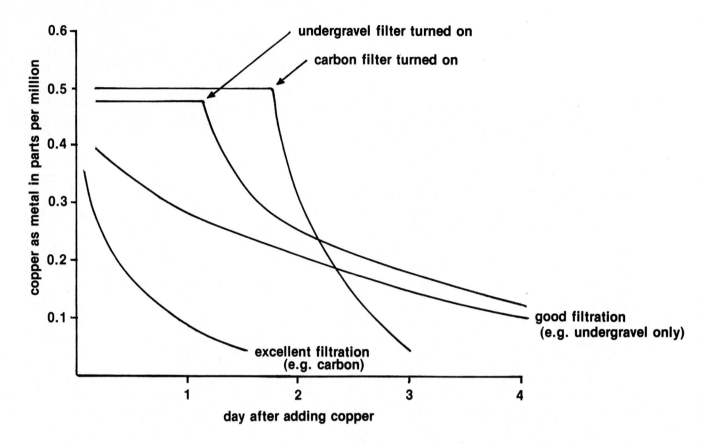

The effects of filtration on copper concentration. "Good" or "excellent" refers only to the removal of toxins and metals, not to normal maintenance. Freely adapted from Miclosz (*Marine Aquarist*, Vol. 3, No. 3, p. 19, 1972).

Trace Elements

These tend to disappear with age of water in the tank. They are taken up by activated charcoal and ion exchange resins, by the fishes and particularly by invertebrates, by plants and to a lesser extent the biological filter. Few meaningful studies have been made of these processes, and it is not clear to what extent ozone or even mechanical filtration may also remove trace elements. Since some of them, at least, are needed for the health of the inhabitants, they must be replaced by water changes, or by adding them periodically to the aquarium. The latter is uncontrolled and could conceivably lead to an unwanted build-up of some elements, although this seems unlikely. By periodic water replacement we are probably maintaining a sub-normal but hopefully sufficient level.

Some trace elements are concentrated to a remarkable extent by particular living organisms. Arsenic, copper, and iodine are good examples, the last-named being concentrated especially by algae. Copper concentration is of importance, as it forms part of the blood pigments of some crustaceans and may be so accumulated by brine shrimp as to render them poisonous to fishes eating them when a tank has been treated with copper in the attempted cure of disease.

Chapter 3

Workable Marine Systems

GENERAL

The heading of this chapter implies that the range of equipment fitted to a particular tank can be expected to keep fishes and/or invertebrates alive for an extended period. To define exactly how long is asking for trouble, since so much depends on species, tank size, skill of the aquarist and a dozen other factors. Perhaps the best definition would be to say that his specimens shall, in general, live for sufficient time for the aquarist to feel that he has had his money's worth! Marine fishes cost plenty if you have to buy all your specimens in an inland city, but very little if you can collect your own. Artificial salts for a big tank are not cheap, but sea water is if you can collect your own or even buy it from a local public aquarium.

Luckily, most of us are optimists where our hobbies are concerned, and often prefer not to check too closely on just how much they are costing us, rather like running a car. The writer has never seen an account of how long fish live in anybody's tanks; perhaps this tells its own story. Public aquaria and zoos do not appear to keep any such statistics regularly either; the latter publish them for mammals and birds but rarely for fishes. Even the warm-blooded vertebrates are considered to be doing reasonably well by most zoos if the annual death rate is below about 40%, so heaven knows what the fish story would be. We must remember that those that live are there as constant reminders of success, while those that

pass on are soon forgotten, and that small birds and mammals don't usually have a very long expectation of life in the best of circumstances, similarly with fishes.

What all this adds up to is that most aquarists would be shocked if they kept careful diaries, but they should, if only to improve their own performance. The writer has been equally shocked when comparing longevity of specimens obtained from different dealers, when it becomes apparent that some sources of supply are very much better than others. These differences may be due to the original methods used to catch and keep the fishes prior to shipment, to how they have been handled since reception by the local dealer, or even to chance similarity between the dealer's tank conditions and those in your own aquarium. As a very general rule, be dissatisfied if most of the fishes you purchase do not live for several months despite what seems to be proper care, hope that they live for a year or two, but don't expect every fish to live for a very long period, as even the best of us have a fair percentage of losses and occasional wipe-outs! This can be true of fresh-water tanks as well as marine ones.

THE "STERILE" SYSTEM ("clinical system")

As the names imply, this system aims at keeping' water as pure as possible and free of disease-causing organisms by mechanical and

The yellow-tailed anemone-fish, *Amphiprion clarkii*, is a widely distributed species extending from the Persian Gulf across the Indo-Pacific to Japan and to Australia. Photo by M. Goto.

The false skunk-striped anemonefish, *Amphiprion perideraion*, is known to enter the gastral cavity of its host anemone without being devoured. Photo by M. Goto.

Bodianus axillaris, the coral hogfish, is a good aquarium fish and it accepts many types of foods. The white spots of juvenile fish (bottom) disappear gradually until completely absent in the adult (top). Top photo by M. Goto, bottom photo by Dr. G.R. Allen.

Sergeant majors, *Abudefduf saxatilis*, are easy to collect in many tropical waters of the world. They are territorial during breeding season. Photo by the New York Zoological Society.

chemical methods. It can certainly be made to work and was, in essence the aim of most early marine fish keepers. It is only as it has dawned on the hobby, trailing behind at least some professionals, that more natural systems are possible, more desirable to many of us, and certainly cheaper, that it has become less of an objective. The fully sterile system does not employ undergravel filters, or if it does, it cleans and changes the bottom layers so frequently that little biological filtration develops, and the filter is merely another coarse mechanical one. Thus, crowded dealer's tanks may use undergravel filtration in a virtually sterile situation, to keep water clear cheaply.

The prime elements in a sterile system are constant coarse and fine filtration, usually in series, so that the water is mechanically polished (as one method phrases it) combined with chemical absorption of soluble material onto charcoal or its oxidation by ozone and/or air stripping. It may also be sterilized by ultraviolet light. All filters need frequent changes every few days or at most every few weeks; water changes are advisable at frequent intervals. Algae may or may not be permitted to grow on corals, usually they are not, and all tank components are taken out and washed clean at frequent intervals, the coral is kept gleaming white and everything is very antiseptic. Against such a clean background the fishes tend to be pale, but this can be alleviated to a fair extent by suitable color decorations and plastic plants which can now be purchased looking quite natural, even in marine aquaria.

The sterile system certainly works, but it is costly and rather unnatural looking, and unless tanks are understocked and large, breakdown of the mechanisms involved can be rapidly fatal. It does have the advantage of immediate utilization of the tanks once they are set up, because it depends on maintenance of water conditions in a suitable (never completely unchanged) state from the start. The water should be beautifully clear if all is well, but frequent checks should be made for the maintenance of acceptable nitrogen cycle components and pH. Despite "sterility" there will be some bacterial action which can cause rapid upset, particularly in a new tank, if it is not being adequately countered by the filters, etc.

The sterile tank, unless utilizing "sterile" undergravel filters, cannot have a deep layer of bottom material, and so it lacks suitability for fishes such as many wrasses which burrow into the substrate. They may adjust, but some appear not to do so very readily. Any depth of sand or gravel beyond about $\frac{1}{2}''$ is courting danger of pockets of anaerobic bacterial growth which results in fouling of the tank and production of gases like hydrogen sulphide (H_2S),

and unsightly black patches in the sand. Hydrogen sulphide is highly toxic and smells abominably of rotten eggs, but it is attacked by ozone, which may help to save the day.

Although the quality of the water in a sterile system may be suitable for invertebrates, other factors are not. Some anemones and crustacea can be kept successfully. Anything which is happy above ground and doesn't feed on algae or is not a filter feeder, but particularly the latter, will not be in trouble. Some have kept filter feeders (bivalve mollusks, many corals and some anemones, sponges, etc.) in sterile systems by having a feeding time when at least the fine filters are turned off and plankton, fine dry food, newly hatched brine shrimp and such are introduced, but it is a difficult business and needs more time devoted to it than most of us can afford. It also tends to clog fine filters very rapidly when unconsumed food is passed through them. However, with

Filter feeders such as the stony coral, gorgonian and tube worms in this tank are more difficult to keep than other invertebrates that feed on larger foods. Photo by R. Straughan.

This very colorful fish is a male *Thalassoma lutescens*, a widely distributed species of wrasse from the Indo-Pacific. Photo by Dr. Shih-chieh Shen.

The bright green fish in this tank is the bird wrasse, *Gomphosus varius*, also known as the longface and beakfish. Wrasses are fast swimmers; they dive into the sand with ease and are difficult to catch. The partially hidden fish is another wrasse (*Thalassoma lutescens*), and the blue fish is a surgeonfish (*Paracanthurus hepatus*). Photo by Dr. Herbert R. Axelrod.

When kept in the aquarium the African clown wrasse, *Coris formosa*, grows without changing to the adult form. Nobody seems to know how. The same is true with some angelfishes. Photo by Dr. Herbert R. Axelrod.

An adult *Coris formosa* photographed by R. Allard. This specimen was captured off the coast of Africa near Mombasa.

Ultra-violet sterilizers, used to prevent and control fish diseases, are available in different models to suit different tank sizes. Courtesy Aquanetics.

ingenuity, time on your hands and a rather deep pocket, it can be done. In summary, the purely sterile system in its various forms is rather like keeping a coronary patient alive in an intensive care ward of a hospital. His chances of survival are much better than if nothing is done for him, but they depend on expensive equipment and constant vigilance. The use of such systems arose from misunderstanding the potential of other methods in the early days of marine aquaria, and misguided advice about running such filters as undergravel and "slow" external filters of various types, which we imagined should be cleaned out at frequent intervals, often before their full functions were allowed to develop. Today, you can, if you choose for some particular reason to do it, run sterile tanks successfully because there is a beautiful range of suitable equipment. One definite advantage of the system is that if it is necessary to treat by drugs or copper, this does not endanger the system, as it would a biological filter in at least some circumstances.

The system, if left on, may render the drug ineffective, but that is another matter.

Biological Filtration

The best and most widely used biological filter in smaller salt-water tanks (i.e. less than a few hundred gallons) is the undergravel filter. Its optimal usage in such tanks has been fairly consistently misunderstood in the past, with the result that some writers have rejected it, on the grounds that it doesn't remove anything from the tank and only helps the solution of waste and hence pollution of the water. Others have recognized its great power as a mechanical filter and the clarity of water attainable with it, but have recommended its partial or total clean-up at frequent intervals. Slowly, we have come to realize that it should be left in place for as long as it goes on working, and even when it clogs up it should only be partially cleaned so as to leave as much as possible of the living bacteria undisturbed. The fully developed biological filter is a living organism—or rather organization—which takes time to develop and is rather easily upset. It is quite unnatural, in the sense that the ocean bed does not have water circulating through it, and the processes going on in the sea, although in part identical with those going on in the biological filter, proceed in a different fashion.

The biological filter, whether of the undergravel type or external to the tank, provides a relatively large mass of material on which bacteria can grow. **This is its essential function.** It doesn't matter what the material is, as long as the water can circulate, adequately, through the body of the filter and be subjected to its bacterial action. By far the most important component of this action is the nitrogen cycle, converting break-down products of nitrogenous waste matter through ammonia and nitrites to nitrates. When it is fully established, the filter's efficiency depends on such factors as the total surface area of its components, its depth, and rate of flow of the water.

The design of such filters should be such as to cause the water in the tank to pass through the filter bed many times a day, slowly through a filter extending over the whole tank bottom and of only a few inches thickness, faster through an external filter with a smaller area but greater depth, if such is used. As long as the filter doesn't clog up too fast, the finer the particle size the better, but the undergravel filter demands a moderate particle size or some of the sand or gravel will pass through below the filter plate and disturb its action. So the base plate should have quite fine slots or holes, and the gravel should be coarse enough to be entirely held back by the plate. It should not be coarser than necessary, however, or it will offer less surface area and also allow uneaten food to pass down into the filter in perhaps dangerous quantities.

The airlift should be highly efficient or insufficient circulation will occur. It should also

Modular power filters allow for expanding the filtering power of a unit simply by adding a new module instead of having to buy an entire new and more powerful filter. Courtesy Rainbow Plastics.

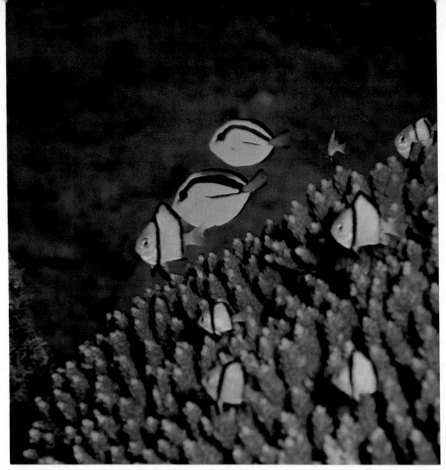

The blue surgeonfish, *Paracanthurus hepatus*, is a very good and tough aquarium fish, much tougher than the powder blue surgeonfish, *Acanthurus leucosternon*. Smaller, vertically striped fishes in the top photo are damselfishes (*Dascyllus*). Top photo by M. Goto. Bottom photo by K.H. Choo.

Another popular fairly hardy fish is the powder blue surgeonfish, *Acanthurus leucosternon*. The species is widely distributed in the Indo-Pacific. Photo by Dr. D. Terver, Nancy Aquarium.

The clown surgeonfish, *Acanthurus lineatus*, is truly an attractive fish on account of its colorful pattern, but it can be a mean customer in the tank also. Photo by Dr. G.R. Allen.

The modular power filters include models powerful enough to filter over 1000 gallons per hour, making them excellent for large tanks. Courtesy Plexitank Engineering.

be accessible, as already noted, so that if it clogs up it is not necessary to burrow down into the gravel and disturb the tank severely in order to deal with it. As the most efficient airlift is a wide, long tube, there should be room to lower an airstone down from the top so that efficiency and ease of servicing are combined. At least, the air line should go down the inside of the airlift, so that its bubbles are released within the base of the tube even if there is not room for an airstone. Most available undergravel filters are not so designed, and offer inefficiency combined with inconvenience in the marine tank. Most were originally designed for fresh-water tanks, where they function more satisfactorily and do not get clogged by salt deposits within the air line. These deposits occur as splash-back happens within the last inch or two of the air line, and are very insoluble and difficult to remove unless you can get directly at them with a wire or hot freshwater. When the air flow starts to fail in an existing set-up of the standard type, try sucking and blowing alternately so as to flush the air

line; it sometimes works. Otherwise, suck the water back and use a siphon action to pass hot fresh water down the air line through into the airlift. Eventually, you will probably have to dismantle the whole wretched arrangement, but with any luck this will put the evil day off for a bit.

Tanks maintained by biological filtration, essentially by an undersand filter in small marine aquaria, differ greatly from those enjoying sterile types of filtration. They depend *primarily* on bacterial action to combat the build-up of products of decomposition and metabolism and must be adequate to do this, or pollution will gradually take over. It is almost impossible to give hard and fast rules for the number of fishes or other inhabitants that any particular arrangement can support; general ones are provided later. Biological filters may be backed up by all kinds of other *secondary* equipment, which should however be unnecessary for maintenance of the tank. For instance, the water may gradually discolor, despite remaining clear, and this may be

THE FILTER BED

removed by activated carbon, which is very good at picking up colored contaminants. Ozone may be used for a similar purpose, and in the early stages to help oxidize nitrogenous products, but if the biological filter is not being overtaxed, these additional measures should hardly be necessary. Airlifts of the right design can move 50–100 gallons per hour and thus circulate the water very effectively, so that a power (water-driven) filter should not be needed, but again, if brisk currents are desired for other reasons, one may be used for the carbon filtration which is probably the best single additional filtering method to add to biological filtration.

A subgravel filter, even if it turns the water in the tank over once or twice per hour, will not cause fast enough water movement at the surface of the filter bed to suck in animal plankton, although it may do so with less active plankton. The importance of this is that filter feeders can exist in the tank if fed on newly hatched brine shrimp or similar active plankton.

In a biological filter, as far as the bacterial action is concerned, it does not much matter what the filter bed is made of, as long as it has the right size of granules, the right depth in relation to granule size, and plenty of surface area for the bacteria to grow on. Activated charcoal would make an excellent bed from this point of view, but few want a black bottom to the tank. Many aquarists aim at the kind of auxiliary action that activated charcoal would have, a simultaneous extra useful function such as absorption of wastes. Whatever the nature of the material, it will be so coated with bacteria after a short period that its secondary function may be severely impaired.

It is fairly generally agreed that a granule size of about $\frac{1}{8}''$ to $\frac{1}{16}''$ is right for an undergravel filter, if smaller it clogs, if much larger food and detritus can travel through it and cause trouble. With such a particle size, a depth of 2″ or 3″ is sufficient for optimal function, as most things happen in the top few inches and deeper gravel is unnecessary, as well as unsightly in all but very large tanks. River

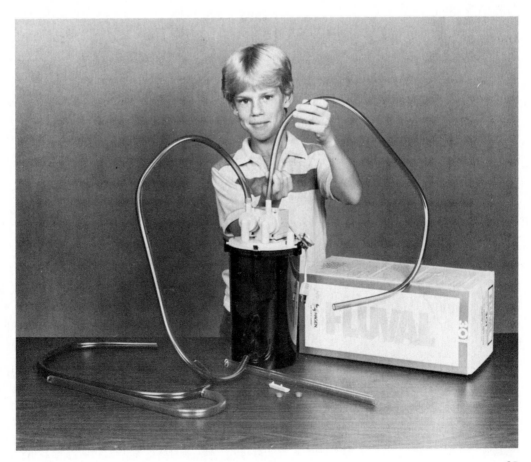

Aquarium manufacturers have designed power filters that consume very little electrical energy in order to perform their filtering functions. Some of the newer models, for example, will filter 100-gallon tanks with only a 10-watt pump unit. Courtesy Rolf C. Hagen Co.

95

Yellow tangs are popular and very common in the reefs of the Hawaiian Islands and widely distributed in the Pacific and Indian Oceans. They eat lots of algae. Photo by Dr. D. Terver.

A yellow tang, *Zebrasoma flavescens,* with an abnormal skin coloration. The individual shown does not represent a new species, as was presumed earlier. Photo by Dr. Herbert R. Axelrod.

A juvenile sailfin tang, *Zebrasoma veliferum*, hovering over a coral reef. Tangs are omnivorous feeders. They will accept brine shrimp and pick on any algae growing in the tank. Photo by M. Goto.

gravel, sea sand (if coarse), silica sand or artificial pads will be neutral in chemical action, whereas coral sand, shell grit, dolomite, limestone or marble are calcareous and offer varying degrees of pH control, depending on their nature and the age of the bed. Generally speaking, the buffering activity is maintained only if a portion of the bed is removed and washed at frequent intervals to get rid of its bacterial, or sometimes phosphate coating. It seems better to rely on the action of coral, which in its turn may get coated, but is easily taken out and washed with a hose.

As the filter bed gets its bacterial coating it also accumulates mulm (detritus) which increases its efficiency and fineness of filtering, but may eventually clog it. It should then be *partially* removed, so as to leave plenty of bacteria in action, and new gravel or washed old gravel returned.

ALGAE

The surface of the filter bed and of the coral, rocks, back and side glasses of the tank are, if adequately lit, going to be coated with green algae. Inadequate lighting promotes brown algal growth, which is unsightly. These algae also perform a useful function and help to complete the cycle going on in the filter, so they should be encouraged as far as possible, and not just thoughtlessly washed off unless they are too profuse. They will be eaten by many fishes and other tank inhabitants, particularly if a day or so of starvation is imposed at intervals. They remove nitrates and many other waste materials otherwise accumulating in the water; unfortunately also trace elements. These are returned to the water if the algae are eaten since much will be voided by the fishes and enter into the cycle once more. Some aquarists collect algae removed because of unsightliness and return it to the tank for this purpose, as

The five tooth-like structures visible on the oral side of the sea urchin are used for scraping algae and other encrusting growths off stones and corals. Photo by G. Marcuse.

A clown surgeonfish, *Acanthurus lineatus*, nibbling algae off a dead coral in the tank. Photo by H. Hansen.

part of the food. There seem to be almost no quantitative studies of the precise contribution of the cycles involving algae, so that some sort of evaluation of their action could be attempted, but there is no doubt that they contribute in particular to reduction of nitrate and phosphate levels and to decreasing the need for as much water changing as would otherwise be necessary. It is striking how rapidly algal growth slows down in a fallow tank with no fishes or invertebrates present, and picks up again when they are re-introduced.

Seddal (Marine Aquarist, **4**, 1, 1973) has studied the effect of algal cultivation (methods regrettably not described) on an established 125 gallon tank with a high nitrate concentration of about 6 mg—as N/liter—which if this author understands correctly, would be about 30 mg NO_3/liter or 30 ppm. Within about 1 month, the nitrate concentration had fallen to around 15 ppm. A similar tank with algae cultivated from the start had only about 7.5 ppm constantly present.

The type or types of algae establishing themselves in a well-lit tank are often fortuitous, but may be influenced by inoculation with a desired strain. Tanks may have bright emerald, drab, or blue-green coatings, the latter tending to blanket everything rather embarrassingly. It is difficult to maintain a mixture of green algae, as one or another usually dominates after a short period, but overall growth can be controlled by light intensity, removal and cleaning of some of the decorations and gravel surfaces periodically, or by active algal feeders.

The internal organs and skin of puffers like this stellate puffer, *Arothron stellatus*, are very poisonous. Photo by Dr. D. Terver, Nancy Aquarium.

All lionfishes should be handled with caution. Poison from the dorsal spines causes extreme pain and swelling. Shown is the whitefin lionfish, *Pterois radiata*, known not only in the Indo-Pacific but also in the Red Sea. Photo by K.H. Choo.

Apparently the goby *Cryptocentrus sungami* shares its burrow with a small shrimp all the time. The shrimp digs the burrow while the goby acts as the watchdog. Photo by M. Goto.

The beautifully patterned tail is the greatest point of attraction of the lace-finned filefish, *Pervagor melanocephalus*. Photo by K.H. Choo.

Sepia officinalis, the common cuttlefish, hides under the sand and it waits for food like small crustaceans, worms and mollusks to come by. Photo by G. Marcuse.

THE NATURAL SYSTEM

Originally advocated by Mr. Lee Chin Eng, of Jakarta, Indonesia, the natural system avoids anything but simple aeration—as seen by the writer, in a tank in the Hotel Indonesia in Jakarta, not even an air-stone was used. The air just bubbled up under large rocks in very large flat bubbles, which looked rather nice and were much in contrast to the fine aeration usually seen. The "natural" tank has a thin-nish layer of sand, rocks and coral in abundance with algae, anemones, worms and other invertebrates forming a quite dense population. This is originally allowed to settle down, and after a few days the fishes are added—not too many, but quite a good population was present in the tank inspected—unfortunately in the absence of Mr. Eng. The idea is that the filter feeders such as bivalves, tube worms and sponges, and other feeders on plankton or fine particulate matter such as many corals can thrive as long as the plankton is not removed, and that in their own way they achieve a balance with algae and fishes and the system survives.

Statistics have just not accumulated to allow a detailed appraisal of this system. Most people who have reported on it (mainly verbally) have stated that it doesn't work, and that sooner or later a drastic collapse occurs and a very smelly wipe-out has to be cleaned up. This is what one must expect, unless very frequent and large changes of water and frequent clean-ups are made, as the nitrifying capacity must be very small and is not being substituted by mechanical and chemical means. The system probably works much better with natural sea

MIXED SYSTEMS

water than with most artificial mixes (see the comparison quoted earlier), but even with natural sea water it would not be expected to show sufficient stability to last for long. It was noted that the tank in Jakarta only contained hardy species of fishes—no chaetodons for example, which are more susceptible to ammonia and nitrites than the average fish. However, until somebody explores the system more thoroughly and takes adequate periodical measurements of pH, ammonia, etc., and explains in detail the maintenance procedures used, we must not be too critical. Perhaps it can be made to work in special circumstances which most of us cannot duplicate—but if this is true, it isn't suitable for most of us to try to use anyway!

A degree of mixing has already been discussed earlier in this chapter, and this section is in part aimed at pointing out some unnecessary or outright incompatible combinations. Thus, the natural system may be fitted out with a subgravel filter and if the rate of flow of the latter is not excessive (it hardly ever will be) the plankton required by the filter feeders will continue to flourish and the tank improved by the presence of the filter. This is sometimes referred to as a semi-natural system, perhaps not a bad name for it. To look at it the other way round, and the most profitable way of proceeding, is to say that to a biologically filtered tank, if by a subgravel filter, may eventually be added a population of invertebrates which will then flourish much more readily than they would without it.

Arrow crabs (*Stenorhynchus seticornis*) are aggressive hunters and are likely to grab and devour small fishes. However, their long spindly legs can easily be bitten off by large fishes. Photo by H. Hansen.

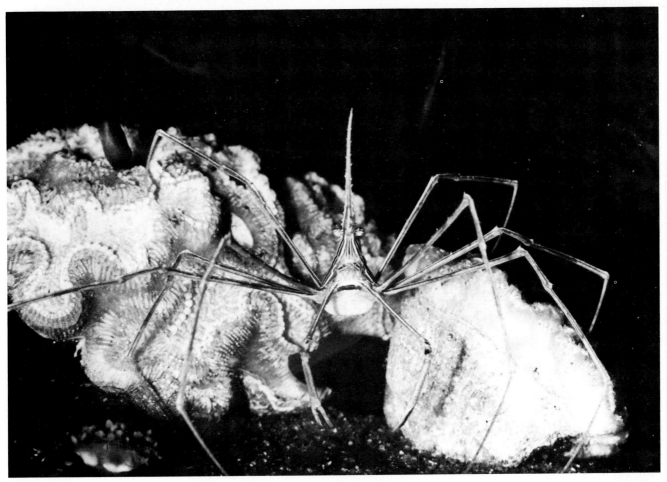

Mr. Lee Chin Eng of Jakarta, Indonesia is the principal proponent of the "Natural System" of salt-water aquarium keeping. Photo by Dr. Herbert R. Axelrod.

Corals with large polyps are easier to keep than those with very minute ones. Foods can be given directly with the aid of a long glass tubing. Photo by Dr. D. Terver, Nancy Aquarium.

Short-spined sea urchins like *Arbacia lixula* from the Mediterranean are very safe to handle. Its spines are not brittle and not likely to get embedded in the skin accidentally. Photo by Dr. K. Knaack.

Staghorn corals (*Acropora*) are fast growers and play a very important role in the process of reef building. *Acropora* species in protected areas are more fragile than those exposed to greater wave and wind action. Photo by Dr. G.R. Allen.

Coral decorations can improve the appearance of a tank, provide shelter to the fish and contribute some dissolved substances to the water. Photo by D. Faulkner.

The simultaneous use of the main elements of sterile filtration, i.e. a coarse and fine external filter, and removal of chemicals in the water and biological filtration is unnecessary and reduces the proper functioning of the biological filter by removing some of its substrates by other means. Only if a tank is grossly overloaded could this be needed, and there are other factors which would dictate that such an overload not be imposed permanently. However, dealers are sometimes faced with such a need, and put in almost everything at once in order to house an unexpectedly large consignment in tanks which do not have the proper capacity to handle it.

Carbon filtration and air stripping with or without ozone is an unnecessary combination, and can cause rapid loss of trace elements, which may cause harm. In general, do not unnecessarily over-treat the water, or you may remove desirable elements without removing any more of the undesirable substances than any one method would do. Ultraviolet irradiation is incompatible with plankton feeding and must be turned off when this is going on—so of course must any fine filtration such as diatomaceous earth or porcelain capsules.

SUMMARY OF FILTERING AND ALLIED METHODS

The following table, reproduced by courtesy of the Marine Aquarium Research Institute of Australia, summarizes the general views of its members on the attributes of the various systems and components we have been discussing:

FILTRATION TABLE

Filters and Media	Mechanical actions	Biological actions	Chemical actions	Efficiency requirements
Subgravel	fair	very good	depends on medium	$\frac{1}{8}''$ particle size, good flow, bacteria
Internal box	good	good	depends on medium	more the better, bacteria
External	good	good	depends on medium	large volume, good flow, bacteria
Micro filters	very good	poor	poor	high pressure pump required
Foam fractionation	good	poor	very good	very small bubbles
Ultraviolet	poor	poor	poor	—
Shell grit	fair	very good	good	as for subgravel
Gravel	fair	very good	none	as above
Nylon wool	good	good	none	bacteria for biological action
Glass wool	very good	good	none	as above
Diatomaceous earth	very good	poor	poor	high pressure pump required
Activated carbon	very good	good	good	bacteria for biological action in addition
Ion exchange	fair	poor	very good	—
Algae	poor	good	slight	remove old algae
Ozone reactor	good	poor	good	very small bubbles
Porcelain	very good	poor	poor	high pressure pump required

The banded coral shrimp *Stenopus hispidus* is well known as a parasite picker. These shrimps, unless a true or mated pair, will fight and maim or kill each other. Fortunately, lost body parts are regenerated in a month or two. Photo by R. Straughan.

This snake-like sea cucumber (*Opheodesoma*) from Hawaii eats detrital matter from the sea floor. Photo by A. Norman.

Provided the disc is unharmed, brittle stars like this *Ophiocoma imbricatus* can grow back any lost arms. Large brittle stars in captivity accept small dead goldfish with real gusto. Photo by A. Power.

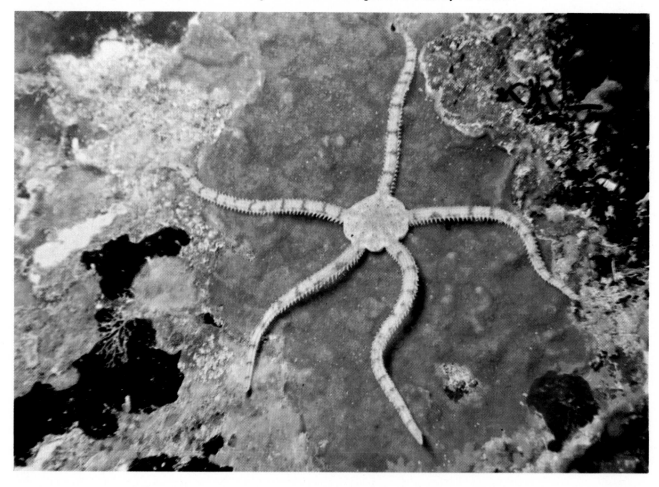

One should avoid contact with the black sea urchin *Diadema setosum* at all times. Its brittle spines are easily broken off and get lodged in the skin causing much pain and possible infection. Photo by A. Power.

The color and pattern of the slate-pencil sea urchin, *Heterocentrotus mammilatus*, vary greatly. Colors range from light pink to brown red in basic coloration with or without stripes across the spines. Photo by Dr. H.R. Axelrod.

Some compatible fishes for a marine tank are shown here: pomacentrids (*Amphiprion*, *Dascyllus*, *Pomacentrus*) and apogonids (longitudinally striped fish). These fishes may inhabit the same general area of the reef also. Photo by Dr. Herbert R. Axelrod.

The present writer is in general agreement with these conclusions, but takes issue with his colleagues on the following:

Internal box filters would have to cover the same area as the aquarium base to be as effective as an undergravel filter, so why the enthusiasm.

Foam fractionation (with or without ozone) can hardly be said to have a good mechanical action although some particulate matter does get swept into the foam.

Ultraviolet light is a sterilizing measure, and so its main action does not come under any of the three headings discussed.

Ion exchange resins probably do not have a beneficial chemical action except to remove unwanted metallic ions, but trace elements presumably go as well.

THE NEW TANK SYNDROME

The tyro starting an aquarium is battling against the odds—not only is it his first venture, but a newly set-up tank is more liable to go wrong than at any other stage. This is doubly true of a sea-water aquarium in which events associated with a settling down period are exaggerated in comparison with the fresh-water tank. These events are particularly tied up with biological filtration, and occur to a lesser degree in a sterile tank—one of its few advantages. Nevertheless, they still do occur, and the advantages of biological filtration already discussed far outweigh the initial difficulties in the long run.

We have noted the nitrogen cycle, which is the cause of the greater part of the new tank syndrome. The tank is set up, aerators and filters are performing nicely by the look of everything, the pH is checked and all is well, so fishes are introduced. In a marine tank, there are several factors making it advantageous to put in a full load of fishes right from the start. They fight less and settle down together; it is easier to purchase them or perhaps have them sent from a dealer all in one batch; and of course everything can be expected to go right if you have followed the instructions or a dealer comes in and sets it all up for you. Then, a few days or a week or two later, in the picturesque words of one writer "*all hell breaks loose.*" The fishes are obviously unhappy, fins droop, they gasp and scratch on rocks and coral, perhaps break out with one disease or another, and if you are really unlucky there are heavy casualties or a complete wipe-out. Had the same fish been placed into a recently vacated old tank, with no previous problems, nothing of the kind would have happened (except for the possibility of their carrying a disease in with them, which often happens but usually it does not break out seriously as in the new tank.)

Why the difference? It is because the old tank would have a nicely balanced bacterial population with the nitrogen cycle proceeding satisfactorily and no build-up of ammonia or nitrites, the villains of the piece. As ammonia is produced it is converted rapidly to nitrites, which in turn are converted to nitrates, which are comparatively non-toxic. Even they are sufficiently removed by algal growth, further conversion to gases which leave the tank, or by the periodic water changes which should be made. The new tank, even if purposely inoculated with some material from an old one, or garden soil, which contains the same bacteria, has an inadequate population of *any* bacteria to keep things moving satisfactorily. The first thing to happen will be a growth of bacteria which decompose organic matter. This may be fish feces, uneaten food, or decaying matter of any kind. The end product of such decomposition is ammonium hydroxide, NH_4OH. In water, there is an equilibrium of the following kind:

$$NH_4OH \rightleftharpoons NH_4^+ + OH^- \rightleftharpoons NH_3 + H_2O.$$

Gobies are hardy and easy to get fishes that can be used for testing the suitability of a tank to support more delicate species later. Photo by Van Raam.

Small individuals of porcupine fish like this *Diodon hystrix* are interesting to observe when they are puffed up. The spines are normally depressed, as seen in the bottom photo. They are extended when any danger is sensed by the fish. Photos by M. Goto.

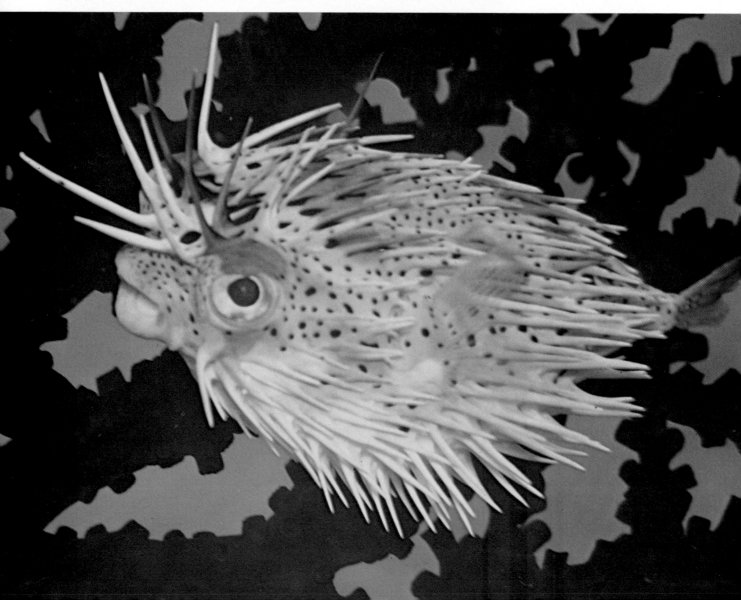

Heniochus acuminatus is sometimes called "the poor man's idol." To a degree it resembles the color pattern of the real Moorish idol, *Zanclus canescens*. Photo by K.H. Choo.

The white patches on
the skin of this olive
surgeonfish, *Acan-
thurus olivaceus*, are
a possible indication
of some kind of
disease. Photo by
G. Marcuse.

The ammonia (NH_3) is the main irritant and toxin, not tolerated by fishes above a fraction of a ppm. The higher the pH, the more ammonia gas is formed—i.e. the equilibrium is pushed towards the right hand side of the equation, hence one reason why sea-water, with a higher pH, is more able to accumulate ammonia gas than fresh-water.

When sufficient ammonium hydroxide accumulates to form a substrate for the growth of bacteria such as *Nitrosomonas*, these will multiply and convert much of it to nitrous acid and nitrites (salts of nitrous acid). So the amounts of NH_4OH and NH_4^+ and NH_3 will fall, but unluckily nitrites are themselves highly toxic and this stage of the cycle on its own doesn't help. When they in turn accumulate sufficiently, other bacteria such as *Nitrobacter* multiply and convert them to nitric acid and ni-

trates (salts of nitric acid). These are not toxic until relatively very high levels are reached, up to 40 or 60 ppm, or hundreds of times the reported toxic levels of ammonia or nitrites. So, in the new tank, we get a wave of ammonia production, lasting for several days or weeks, according to conditions, followed as it subsides by a wave of nitrite production, lasting for up to several weeks or even months, followed by subsidence of nitrites and a lasting high level of nitrates which unless excessive, does no harm. This part of the nitrogen cycle is the *nitrification* stage. Other bacteria work in the reverse direction, and would be stimulated to grow if nitrates were added to the original water, but nobody wants that. Instead, the main cycle proceeds by further bacterial action to a rebuilding of complex compounds, but most such processes are accomplished by plants, by algae in the marine tank. Some plants can utilize ammonia, but the cycle depends in the main on the bacterial transformations described.

How do we avoid the new tank syndrome? Ideally, by converting it to an old tank before introducing precious coral reef fishes, or by the gradual introduction of the fish population. Either method has its disadvantages; method one means perhaps a couple of months of using the tank for turtles or tough fishes such as eels or catfish before using it for its intended purpose. Method two means waiting to build up the fish population and taking greater risks of fighting and injury. Either is safer than to risk the effects of the new tank syndrome on delicate species. Ozone oxidizes both ammonia and nitrites efficiently, but if it is introduced to a tank intended eventually to be biologically filtered, it will only hinder the build-up of desirable bacteria and prevent rapid or even effective nitrification. It acts only slowly on nitrates, so the end effect of ozone treatment is also nitrate accumulation, and a rapid rise in ammonia when the ozone is turned off. The growth of a suitable bacterial population in the biological filter depends on ammonia and nitrite formation to stimulate growth and continued functioning of the relevant organisms, and thus the new tank must be allowed to pass through the build-up phases of toxic products in order to arrive at a stable state in which NH_3 and NO_2 levels are almost nil.

How do we know when a tank is in biological equilibrium? By measuring the ammonia, nitrite and nitrate concentrations. The first two should be virtually nil, the third should not exceed about 40 ppm, preferably 20 ppm unless only tough fishes are being housed. Any really

A tank can be aged by keeping some marine catfish (*Plotosus anguillaris*) in it for a couple of months. Catfish are easy to care for and not at all prohibitive in cost. Photo by H. Hansen, Aquarium Berlin.

The angelfishes illustrated on these pages are very popular, colorful and good aquarium fishes, except for *Centropyge bicolor* which is rather touchy.

Centropyge flavissimus. Photo by Dr. Herbert R. Axelrod.

Centropyge heraldi. Photo by K.H. Choo.

Holacanthus tricolor.
Photo by Dr. J.E.
Randall.

Centropyge bicolor.
Photo by Dr. G.R. Al-
len.

It is good practice to keep the three-spot damselfish, *Dascyllus trimaculatus*, in an aquarium containing a large branching coral. They hide in between the branches of the coral or stay close to large sea anemones for protection in their natural habitat. Photo by G. Marcuse.

measurable rise in NH_3 or NO_2 concentration spells danger—actually, about 0.1 ppm and 0.25 ppm respectively—and should be combated by reducing the fish concentration, increasing the rate of turnover of new sea-water, and attending to tank hygiene in general, such as overfeeding, decaying material under rocks or in corners which is not getting dealt with adequately or insufficient aeration and water movement. In a new tank, NH_3 and NO_2 levels can easily rise to 5 or 10 ppm, so expect high measurements if the settling down period is not over.

MANAGEMENT OF BIOLOGICAL FILTERS

A biological filter is a living community, consuming oxygen and containing vast numbers of organisms that can die and foul the water instead of purifying it. They will die if under-oxygenated, poisoned or subjected to prolonged antibiotic or disinfectant treatment. If under-nourished, such as when the fish population is removed, they appear to rest rather than die off unless perhaps left for very long periods.

Lack of oxygen, as when the air pump fails with an undergravel filter, has been said by some authors to be followed by serious consequences in a few hours, even as little as two hours. Perhaps this can be so in some circumstances, but the present writer has not discovered serious consequences in a normally populated tank even with a 24 hour stoppage. In fact, this technique is actually used to see if the tanks are in good shape—if the fishes appear unstressed when everything is turned off for a day, all is well. There is no doubt, however, that more prolonged failures are highly dangerous, even fatal in crowded tanks, when rapid depletion of oxygen would occur with accumulation of waste products. In a small, overstocked tank, whether filtered biologically or otherwise, rapid and serious consequences can occur within a few hours—a good reason already given for not using such tanks.

It would seem that conventional amounts of copper, so frequently used as a disease cure in marine tanks, are not particularly dangerous to a biological filter, although measurements of what is happening to the bacteria do not seem to have been made. One conjectures that larger amounts, or such measures as a copper drip often used in public aquaria, indeed any way by which the concentration of copper would be maintained for prolonged periods, might well be much more dangerous. Similar observations would hold for most species of algae; a single copper treatment of up to 0.4 ppm metallic Cu^{++} does not usually worry them, but repeated treatments do, and algal decay may become a menace in the tank.

With antibiotics a different story is met, at least on some occasions. The wide spectrum antibiotics are particularly dangerous and their use can lead to prolonged depression of the action of an undergravel filter and distress to the tank inhabitants, which may suffer worse consequences than would have followed the disease for which they were treated. There are various methods by which the fishes can be treated with antibiotics without serious risk to the filters, and these are discussed later.

We have seen that a biological filter should remain undisturbed as long as possible. Taking

The behavior of the yellowhead jawfish, *Opisthognathus aurifrons*, as it constructs its burrow is very fascinating. They regularly rearrange the small rocks and pebbles that surround the opening of the burrow. Photo by G. Marcuse.

Good marine fishes for beginning hobbyists are the blue devils, the popular name applied to many species of blue pomacentrids like *Abudefduf cyanea*, shown here. Photo by K.H. Choo.

Fish shipments from the Far East usually include some dusky angelfishes, *Centropyge bispinosus*. These fish accept prepared food, especially if some algae is included. Photo by Dr. Herbert R. Axelrod.

The eye spot on the dorsal fins of the ocellate damselfish *Pomacentrus vaiuli* is one of the characters useful to scientists for its identification. Photo by M. Goto.

Amphiprion ocellaris is the anemonefish most commonly sold in the United States. It was the first of its kind bred in captivity and thrives even in the absence of its host anemone. Photo by R. Straughan.

it down and washing the gravel removes so many bacteria that their action is seriously impaired, and of course replacing the old gravel with new starts the whole filter virtually from scratch again. As the top layers of the filter get filled by debris—itself a bacterial bed and a fine filter medium—it may slow the passage of water excessively. So scratch it around a bit and help to loosen things up, but don't remove anything unless the actions of the fishes are causing persistent cloudiness as they move around the bottom of the tank. If this occurs, siphon off much of the loose debris and perhaps some of the top gravel, but leave most of the gravel to keep up the good work. Wash gently and replace the gravel removed, do not scour

it clean, and prefer such re-use to new gravel. By such methods a tank may remain without complete overhaul for many years and be the better for it. If a complete overhaul becomes imperative, replace the old gravel without more washing than is necessary, so as to start off with as good a bacterial population as is possible. The same applies to algae, etc., on rocks and coral in a biologically maintained tank. Never scour everything clean; brighten up the tank by periodical replacement or part washing of some of the decorations, but never all at once. Very attractive effects can be achieved with a mixture of clean, half-clean and algae-covered materials. A "clinical" tank has clinical looking fish—pale and hospital-like.

Chapter 4

Handling Fishes and Invertebrates

TANK CAPACITY

We now have a tank ready to receive fishes. Whether we feel able to put them all in at once, or intend to build up gradually, how many fishes can the tank be expected to hold? A first answer is *very much fewer* than in the corresponding fresh-water tropical tank. Rules of thumb like so many inches per gallon or per square foot of surface area do not hold for marines. So much depends on the particular system chosen and the individual conditions of a tank and its intended inhabitants that a mixture of guidance and experience is the best that can be offered. The best environment for marine fishes is a large, underpopulated tank, in which many species will survive happily for surprisingly long periods: The worst environment is a small tank of a few gallons capacity with five or ten medium sized fishes (1″ to 2″ in body length, exclusive of the tail fin) which can be maintained successfully only by an experienced marine aquarist willing to give frequent attention to ensure that all is well. A few hours of equipment breakdown, or a day or two of neglect—and disaster, particularly with artificial salt-water.

With that warning, the author will now proceed to give some rules which are intended purely for guidance only, no guarantees! For reasonable safety, and to be pretty sure that there is no overcrowding, in an established conditioned tank, or one very adequately serviced by mechanical and chemical filtration under the clinical system, there should initially be only one fish of 1″ to 2″ in length per 5 gallons of water. This allows for growth of the fishes, which will occur quite rapidly under such conditions, so that in a few months there will be one fish of 2″–4″ length per 5 gallons, at which stage they will either be adult and not likely to grow much more, or they will start to be slowed down by a crowding factor and tank size limitations the full operations of which are very poorly understood. All one can say is that small tanks do not allow full growth of the fishes, nor does crowding in a large tank. If you are an experienced aquarist willing to give frequent water changes and to supervise events in the aquarium to a greater extent than average, you can exceed these limits, but *never* to a greater extent than, say, one fish initially of up to 3″ in length or in a stable situation of up to 4″ in length per 3 gallons, but not all fishes to be at the limit of size—i.e. mix 1″ to 4″ fishes in a 50 gallon tank with a limit of 16–18 fishes. If all were 4″ in length, it would be a risk to exceed say 12 fishes. The allowance drops rapidly with increasing size, so that only 4–6 fishes of 6″ and only 2 or 3 at 8″–9″ could be housed, and these allowances are for experienced aquarists—halve them otherwise! The rules also need flexibility depending on species, but not very much. It is feasible to crowd tough customers such as lionfish, sargassum fish and catfish to a greater degree than chaeto-

This spectacular looking but non-predatory anemone, *Metridium marginatum*, is native to the Northeast Pacific. It eats small foods like brine shrimp, *Tubifex*, plankton, etc. Photo by U.E. Friese.

Lysmata grabhami, a cleaning shrimp from the Atlantic, Pacific, and Indian Oceans, is just as popular as the banded coral shrimp *Stenopus hispidus*. Photo by R. Jonklaas.

This pretty red shrimp comes from Hawaii. It definitely can add some color to a tank, but one should not place crustacean-eating fishes with it. Photo by A. Norman.

This particular specimen of *Pterois volitans* was incredibly long-lived. It lived for six years, a record its keeper can be proud of. Photo by R. Straughan.

dons or angelfishes, but in a mixed tank the former will probably survive while the others decline and die if too many are crowded together.

SELECTION OF FISHES

The selection of suitable fishes falls under two main headings—how to select healthy young fishes, and how to combine compatible species in one tank. The first important step is the purchase of healthy specimens, which should also be only part-grown and not ready to die a natural death soon after you have acquired them. In fact, the latter is rarely a problem, since collectors and dealers prefer to ship large numbers of immature fish rather than a few large older ones.

A healthy young fish is well below the textbook quoted size, shows immature or early adult color and markings if it is of a species which changes with age (and many do), and

looks alert, with relatively slow, unexaggerated gill movements. Its fins should be erect, its color bright, but not intense or very dark, as this may be a sign of approaching demise. There should be no sign of disease, no scratching or flipping of the body suggesting irritation, no glancing off rocks or coral. Ask the supplier to feed the fishes you wish to buy, and observe them eating. Be wary of any that do not accept food, unless they have a full abdomen and the dealer asserts that they were recently fed. On no account buy a thin fish, or one with a hollow belly. Look at *all* the fishes in a dealer's tank, and do not buy a healthy looking specimen if others in the tank are unhappy or appear suspicious in any way. Slight fin or tail damage, as long as it is not accompanied by inflammation or other signs of trouble, may be accepted since marine fishes are very aggressive, and a degree of bickering and damage must be expected.

Many dealers assert that they quarantine their fishes for an adequate period; perhaps some really do, but very many don't. It is also a debatable point how much good this does unless the dealer is a first class marine aquarist. If he isn't, it is probably best to get them as soon as possible and quarantine them yourself if facilities are available. Unfortunately, it is rarely possible to receive them straight into your own tanks without their receiving a baptism in his, and this is where the damage may be done. It isn't much use, for instance, for a careful customer to take newly purchased fishes home and to transfer them with all care by stages into his own water, with attention to pH, salinity and temperature changes, if they were received by the dealer yesterday and dumped straight into his tanks with no care at all.

If you are buying a batch of fishes intended as community inhabitants of a conditioned (or sterile) tank, they will do best if they are all put in together, with a careful watch on subsequent events. They are all new to their sur-roundings, haven't exerted any territorial rights or peck order yet, and with any luck will settle down peacefully. Nevertheless, don't expect large angels to accept one another very readily, or some of the wrasses. Two fish of the same species are also liable to bicker or even fight to the death, so that the common fresh-water habit of purchasing a "pair" is usually not best for the marine aquarium. Even if things seem right originally, one will often start persecuting the other and cause it to lose condition. This is seen with many species— chaetodons, clowns, chelmons, demoiselles and of course almost all angels. Some species will do better in larger groups; a pair is about the worst to risk. Don't be mislead by the fact that these fishes seem to be peaceful in the dealer's tanks, where they are often crowded into bare receptacles and disturbed so frequently that they do not have the chance to establish domin-ance or territorial relationships and thus to start quarrelling in earnest. It is when you get them home into a tank where they can settle

Except for the suspicious spot near the tail, the fish pictured, a powder blue surgeonfish (*Acanthurus leucosternon*) may be desirable. However, small blemishes can be a source of trouble later. Photo by K. Paysan.

With growth the process on the forehead of *Heniochus varius* becomes more pronounced, so the species has earned the common name humphead bannerfish. Photo by K.H. Choo.

Most boxfishes after a period of time in captivity become very tame and react to the presence of man near by. The spotted cube, *Ostracion cubicus*, is an attractive boxfish from the tropics. The juvenile (top) has much darker spots than the adult (bottom). Photos by M. Goto.

An upturned clam shell provides fishes with a natural looking shelter. It is easy to remove for cleaning also. Photo by R. Straughan.

down with plenty of room and nooks and crannies to call their own that they will develop full belligerence.

If your tank is new and unconditioned, yet you wish to start the gradual introduction of fishes, start with the smaller and more peaceful types first. They will become bolder as they settle in, and when others are introduced, even innately fiercer and larger specimens may settle down without worrying the established inhabitants much—they may even suffer themselves for a while, but will usually not be too adversely affected. Of course, there will be exceptions and a watch must still be kept, but it is surprising how a community may be built up by such methods. Another way is to introduce new fishes together with a change of scenery, so that old and new alike are presented with unfamiliar surroundings. You can rearrange old decorations or introduce some new ones, but make the change quite big, not just the juggling of a few pieces. This is often the only practical way of introducing new small fishes to an established tank, otherwise they may need to be protected by a barrier or by immersing them in an adequate receptacle for a day or two so that the old inhabitants get tired of banging their noses and can perhaps be trusted from then on.

HANDLING NEW FISHES

We have just discussed the *strategy* of fish introduction, but not the details. If the fishes are in water which differs in any of a variety of ways from that in the tank for which they are destined, it may be fatal or severely detrimental to dump them straight into it. Sudden changes in pH, specific gravity, temperature and nitrogenous matter content can all cause shock, susceptibility to disease, or even rapid death within a few minutes. Gradual changes will often be tolerated quite readily, the speed of acclimatization depending on magnitude and species.

Upward temperature changes are fairly readily tolerated if the fish or invertebrate is *below* the normal temperature range, indeed it has been found better to rush chilled fishes into warm water than to do it gradually. Temperatures *above* the normal for semi-tropical species are not advocated as a permanent feature, but in any case such changes should be made very gradually. Sudden upward changes *within* the normal range (say 20°–30°C or 68°–86°F) should not exceed 3°C (5°F). Downward temperature changes should never be extreme and should not in general exceed a sudden 1.5°C (3°F) or that amount per day in greater changes. If you can take your time over cooling or heating a tank, don't exceed 1°C (2°F) per day. Also, don't worry if the Centigrade and

Fahrenheit figures given are not exactly in correspondence; they are all convenient approximations, meant as a series of guides only.

Changes in specific gravity (salinity) should also be kept within limits. Again, upward changes occurring within the naturally tolerated range, which for most purely marine (stenohaline) fishes is about 1.017 to 1.030, can be somewhat greater than downward (more dilute) changes. A change of about 0.0025, say a 10% change on average, is the maximum sudden change, or recommended daily change. There was a fad for keeping marines in more dilute water than average—i.e. at about 1.017 rather than 1.025, but this is questionable and somewhere between 1.022 and 1.027 would seem wise. Remember however that 1.022 at 80°F is 1.025 approximately at 60°F, thus at 80°F the range would be 1.019 to 1.024 approximately.

Changes in pH are best kept within about 0.2, either sudden or per day. This is a *percentage* change in H^+ ion concentration of about 60%, a full pH change of 1.0 being a 1000% change—i.e. pH 7.0 to pH 8.0. While it has been found that little harm in an established tank seems to follow if the pH drops to as low as 7.0, it does not mean that you can suddenly transfer fish at pH 8.3 without risk. Hardy ones, yes, but delicate species may be killed! This is one reason why a tank (or circulating system) should not be allowed to drop much below the range usual in the sea—i.e. around 7.8 to 8.5. The difficulty of introducing new specimens is then much lessened.

Offering the latticed butterflyfish, *Chaetodon rafflesi*, some live coral and small invertebrates will be a real treat. However, they are known to do well with a diet of freeze-dried brine shrimp and frozen fish food also. Photo by G. Marcuse.

The leopard grouper, *Cromileptes altivelis*, during its early life appears more attractive than when it is fully grown. The large spots eventually become very much reduced in size. Like any other grouper it will eat other fishes. Photo by H. Hansen.

One has plenty of opportunity to appreciate the beauty of the cardinal fish *Sphaeramia nematopterus*. It is not prone to hiding and usually stays almost motionless in the water with all the fins spread out. Photo by G. Claude.

Very few persons will have the privilege of seeing live individuals of the damselfish *Paraglyphidodon polyacanthus*. They are found in Norfolk and Lord Howe Islands near Australia, areas too remote for aquarium dealers in this country. Photo by R. Steene.

The three-spot angelfish *Apolemichthys trimaculatus*, also called flag angel by others, has two important features which maintain its popularity. It is an attractive and hardy fish. Photo by Dr. G.R. Allen.

Tolerance to ammonia, nitrites and other toxic substances can build up in some fishes to a level which is intolerable to others which are suddenly introduced to it. Thus there are many factors which must be taken into account when moving fishes around. If it is convenient, measure those mentioned as a surer guide to procedure than chance. If it isn't, always mix the water in which the fishes have been residing in a series of steps with that into which they are going. Very often only 30 or 60 minutes with 2 or 3 steps will take care of the differences adequately, and can be achieved by floating large jars in the tank, or by siphoning the tank water by stages into the bags or carrier containing the new arrivals. If differences are great, more elaborate precautions such as a temporary large plastic bag or tank with heating and aeration may be needed and the change-over may take one or more days. A lot of fishes are lost through neglect of these precautions.

Physical contact with fishes should be avoided, for your sake and theirs. Quite a number have poison spines or can give painful wounds or bites. Damage to the fish is also likely. Poor technique with nets can easily damage fishes, particularly those with spines likely to get caught in the mesh. Where possible, it is best eventually just to tip or pour them gently into the aquarium. If there are inhabitants already in the tank, do it after feeding them and in a dim light; both are factors which favor a peaceful introduction!

The natural food of this polka dotted shrimp (*Hymenocerus*) is the tube feet of starfish. They do not appear to fare too well with substitutes. Photo by H. Hansen.

The cleaner wrasse *Labroides dimidiatus* accepts dry foods but will also pick on the skin of other fishes; one is shown here "cleaning" a butterflyfish (*Chaetodon collare*). Photo by H. Hansen.

INVERTEBRATES

Some invertebrates are tougher than most fishes, some are very much more tender, and are difficult to maintain. Unless you are an experienced marine aquarist it is much better to set up a separate tank for them, as some of the conditions in which they will do best are bad for the fishes, and to an extent the reverse holds true. It is also difficult to treat fishes for disease in the presence of invertebrates as some of the most effective measures, such as copper treatment, are rapidly fatal to most invertebrates.

The natural system with no artificial filtration is more suited to most invertebrates than to fishes, but it cannot accommodate deep sand or gravel, which will go black and smelly, and is not suited to burrowing forms. It relies on filter feeders for its filtration, but if these are too successful they will starve unless there are continual additions of suitable food or plankton—the latter not feasible for most of us. This food is liable to accumulate in undisturbed corners and be a nuisance. Thus, even with invertebrates alone the natural system is not all it might be, and a carefully managed undergravel, biological filter seems best. If it is not overtaxed and violently aerated, the rate of travel of water is not such as to filter off plankton-like material at all rapidly, and creatures like newly hatched brine shrimp, which swim up towards the light, are not removed by it. It is, therefore, possible to feed filter feeders even in the presence of a working undergravel filter, and at most it might be found necessary to turn it off for an hour or two while the filter feeders consume their dinner. This short stoppage will not harm the biological filter.

One of the small crustaceans found in the reefs around the Hawaiian Islands is the spiked prawn (*Saron*). The hair-like tufts on the back and on the front legs are female characteristics. The males have very long front legs without tufts. Photo by A. Norman.

Small individuals of the spiny lobster *Panulirus ornatus* can be decorative and easy to keep besides. They are nocturnal omnivores who graze on algae and lower invertebrates, seldom attack large prey. Photo by A. Norman.

All hermit crabs like this *Paguristis ocellatus* will periodically need larger mollusk shells to replace the old shells after each molting. As mentioned elsewhere, hermit crabs are destructive and should be kept by themselves. Photo by Dr. K. Knaack.

The hermit crab *Pagurus predauxi* and its commensal sea anemone *Adamsia palliata* both eat the same type of food. In the wild state the anemone subsists on food left uneaten by the hermit crab. Photo by U.E. Friese.

Like most other starfishes, this *Astropecten* will feed on clams, mussels, etc. Given this type of diet they'll thrive in captivity. However, they are very dependent on the pH, which should not be less than 8.0. Photo by G. Marcuse.

Other biological or mechanical filters, with a rapid throughput and consequent efficient removal of suspended materials will clean up the water too fast for the filter feeders and are unsuitable for continued use in a tank containing them. At best, they may be used intermittently, with the danger that any filter with a biological component—such as a charcoal filter not frequently renewed—is liable to go bad and discharge toxins when turned on again if left off for too long. How long is too long? It all depends on conditions—a few hours in an overtaxed system or a really deep-layer filter, up to a day or two in an undertaxed relatively thin-layered undergravel filter.

Invertebrates consume oxygen just as do fishes, but it is difficult to make hard and fast rules about tank capacities. The less active invertebrates, such as anemones, corals, mussels and sessile forms in general consume less

oxygen than their size or body weight (of living material) might suggest, and quite a display can be housed in a medium-sized aquarium. Crabs, nudibranchs, univalve mollusks and various other moving forms consume more oxygen, while squids, octopuses and similarly very active invertebrates need better aeration and more room than the average fish. They also tend to be very sensitive to ammonia and nitrite levels, which have to be kept down even lower than the next-to-zero requirements for fishes. This may demand better than average filtration, and in at least some circumstances ozone has been found very helpful. The author has seen tanks kept under a more or less natural system with a preponderance of invertebrates of very mixed nature respond quite remarkably to ozone, administered through an air-stripping device. With the ozone off, cockles, small octopuses, corals and other forms drooped within a few hours, recovering quite rapidly when it was switched on again. However, these tanks did not have biological filtration or carbon filters, both of which would have helped, and other aquaria so equipped seem to be maintained successfully without ozone. The situation, like many others in this area, needs further research.

A new tank, or new water, is often unsuited to invertebrates just as to fishes, unless managed in a similar manner to that suggested above. No doubt their frequent high sensitivity to toxic nitrogenous compounds is a big factor. Even in the natural system, new water with its rapid rise in bacterial count, seems liable to defeat the filter feeders and to be unsuited to them. An invertebrate tank should therefore be handled much the same as one for vertebrates, in its initial stages and also later on, but with even greater attention to keeping pollutants down and oxygen levels up. We have already seen that artificial mixes must be of a very high grade for the maintenance of invertebrates, otherwise at least half of the water should be natural sea water. They are much more dependent on trace elements than fishes—which get a lot of things in their diet that it is more difficult to supply to other phyla except through the water. The actual trace elements measurably accumulated by invertebrates differ greatly from one species to another, but it is not usually known whether such accumulation is necessary to the animal which performs it. An important point is that the elements in question are being removed, and if some other creature needs them he will be unlucky. So an invertebrate tank needs more frequent renewal of water than a pure fish tank, or as techniques develop, more frequent monitoring and additions of trace elements themselves.

Cylinder sea anemones (*Cerianthus*) are beautiful but very toxic. They can kill by contact other anemones and coral. Photo by A. Holtman.

Looking through one of the siphons of this tunicate one can see the intricate feeding mechanism of this little-known animal. Tunicates are not rare animals, but they are quite small and generally drab in coloration and can be easily ignored. Casual collectors are rarely successful in keeping them. Very little is known about their biological requirements. Photo by Dr. G.R. Allen.

Odontodactylus scyllarus is representative of a small group of crustaceans called mantis shrimps. Mantis shrimps are predatory and prefer live food but other fresh foods like chopped fish and clams are also eaten. This particular species is quite colorful and does not grow as large as mantis shrimps of the genus *Squilla*. Photo by M. Goto.

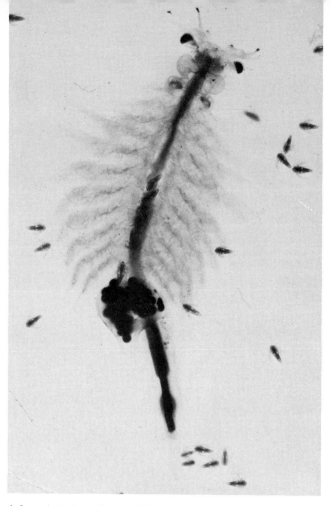

A female brine shrimp. Photo by Dr. C.W. Emmens.

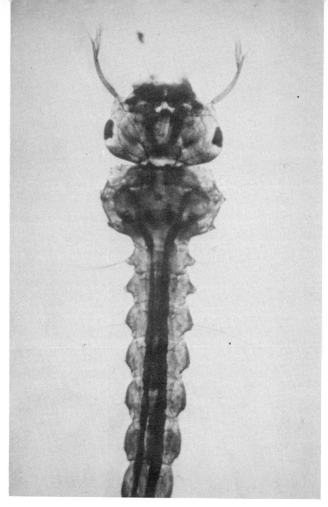

A mosquito larva. Photo by Dr. R. Geisler.

FEEDING FISHES

Marine fish have very healthy appetites, heartier than the general run of fresh-water fishes, and must be fed adequately and frequently if they are really to flourish. Most of them are not choosey, and will eat dry food, frozen or freeze-dried foods and of course live food with great relish. Whether the food always contains sufficient and suitable nourishment is another matter, and care must be taken to see that foods appropriate to all tank inhabitants are being supplied. Some marines are difficult to feed, outstandingly some of the chaetodons, file fishes, and pure predators such as lionfishes or anglerfishes. Luckily, many of the latter will learn to take dead material such as prawns and strips of fresh fish, but some species are not so obliging. Also, if it is necessary to teach them to eat such food, an interesting spectacle in the tank is lost—the chase by the lionfish and its spreading fins which herd its prey like a net, and the display by the anglerfish of its wriggling

worm-like bait to attract the passing victim. However, inland aquarists must be grateful that such elegant species can be maintained at all, far from the sea and their natural prey.

If one observes fishes on a coral reef, they are seen to be continually picking at their food. Only the predators feed at infrequent intervals; for the others it is a perpetual feast as long as daylight lasts. We cannot fully imitate these conditions in an aquarium, but it must be stressed that small and young fishes cannot eat enough once or twice a day for full nourishment and adequate growth. They must be fed several times daily and if possible a little excess food should be around so that they can pick at it for a while at least. It is not impossible to arrange this, although care must clearly be exercised not to foul the water or to overtax the system. Live food is clearly a good solution —newly hatched brine shrimp, mosquito larvae, algae are all examples of foods which do not cause pollution unless they die off before being eaten because of toxins or because they are collected and killed in filters. Some flake foods do not pollute the water and can also, with caution, be fed in mild excess so as to leave some pickings. There are also a few preparations around intended to provide for such continuous feeding, but the author has not been too successful with the one or two tried out—perhaps you may be more so.

Large fishes do all the better for frequent feeding, but they do not demand it to the same extent. They will survive and grow a little on twice daily feeding, as their stomachs can hold more in proportion to their total requirements per day at one feeding. If you cannot feed frequently, be wary of trying to keep specimens less than 1½″ to 2″ long, particularly small immature members of species that eventually grow quite large. Chaetodons of less than about 2″ in length are particularly troublesome and often fail to survive for more than a few weeks

if not given frequent feeds or constant live food. This does not mean that well-fed fishes cannot survive a period of starvation, they can. Plump young fish can go for 2 or 3 days without harm, and well-fed older fishes for a week or even longer. What they cannot stand is prolonged underfeeding which keeps them undernourished and thin and prone to disease and deformity.

For those who live near the sea, it is a great temptation to feed live marine foods—algae, "live" rocks for picking over, small crustacea and plankton, and for larger fishes, small shrimps and other fish or their fry. This is hazardous and regrettably likely to cause disease, because marine organisms may carry marine-fish diseases. Live foods from freshwater are much safer, but never completely safe since some bacterial diseases are common to fresh- and salt-water, probably some other diseases are too. However, even tubifex worms, well washed, are fairly safe and probably better than no live food at all. Healthy fishes aren't

In nature the splitlure frogfish, *Antennarius scaber*, uses its lure to attract unsuspecting fishes and other animals, which are then quickly swallowed. Photo by the New York Zoological Society.

A dramatic illustration of the huge mouth of the lionfish *Pterois volitans*. Photo by M. Goto.

A lizardfish (*Synodus*) in the act of swallowing its food. Lizardfishes are bottom dwellers and very active hunters in the reef. Photo by M. Goto.

A school of goatfishes (*Mulloidichthys samoensis*) photographed while feeding. The barbels are used for feeling the presence of live food beneath the sea floor. Photo by A. Power.

Appetite stimulants can be used to provide essential vitamins while coaxing finicky fishes into eating well. Courtesy Hawaiian Marine Imports.

going to catch everything going even if it is introduced to the tank. Newly hatched or cultured brine shrimp are about as safe as one can get, so are mosquito larvae, *Daphnia*, white worms or microworms, all of which will live long enough in the marine aquarium to get eaten unless fed in gross excess. Fresh-water algae, scraped from a tank, or of the hair-like variety, are relished by many marines, although they may have to learn to like them initially.

Those who cannot readily get marine live food can take consolation therefore, even those who cannot get any live food at all, except as a rare treat, need not despair, as modern prepared foods and what you yourself can prepare in the kitchen can form a perfectly adequate

diet for many species without their ever receiving any actual living food. This is especially so if a vitamin supplement is given, and several are now available for fishes. A staple food mix for a community tank can be prepared from chopped clams, scallops, lean meat or beef heart, shrimps, prawns or crab meat—the last three preferably cooked for sterility. Chop according to size range of fishes and make up in batches which will last for 1–2 weeks, preferably in ice-cube containers for convenience in handling. Wash well either before storage or after thawing, and store in the deep-freeze part of the refrigerator. To this add chopped deep-frozen lettuce outer (green) leaves, spinach, peas or other green vegetables according to the needs and taste of the fishes—surgeons, angels, wrasses and other predominantly vegetable feeders will need plenty, and all fishes but outright predators should take some. It is a curious and often neglected fact that nearly all marine fishes are slow to accept fresh land-grown vegetables, however finely minced, but will readily take them after freezing. When they are thawed out, they are mushier and certainly seem more like the marine algae to which the fish are accustomed, perhaps that's the reason. To the meat and plant offering, add deep-frozen brine shrimp or canned Norwegian brine shrimp, particularly for younger and smaller fishes. Just before feeding, a few drops of a vitamin preparation can be added, but don't overdose.

The fresh food mix above can be alternated with a good brand of flake food, freeze-dried foods such as brine shrimp, tubifex and *Daphnia*,

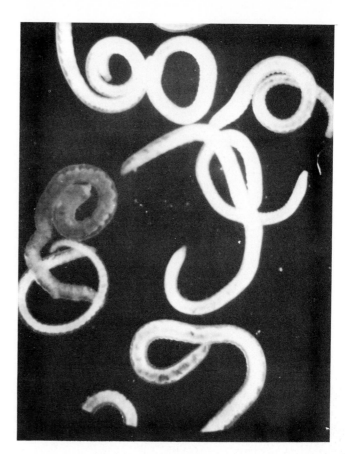

Commercially prepared foods have been developed to make the feeding of filter-feeding and particle-feeding marine invertebrates easier and less chancy. Courtesy Hawaiian Marine Imports.

Another live food that marine fishes seem to like are white worms (*Enchytraeus*). The worms can survive in sea water for several hours, so the fishes have more opportunity to eat them later. They can also be chopped very finely for smaller fishes. Photo by Dr. R. Geisler.

or dried shrimp, turtle food or the like for larger fishes. They love nearly all of these prepared foods, which should always be fed to them some of the time to keep up a well mixed diet and to keep the fishes ready to eat as large a variety of foods as possible, in cases of any shortages or hurried feedings. If good algal growth is also present in the tank, the fishes should really flourish on the types of diet just discussed, and will be able to pick at algae covered rocks and coral in between frequent light feedings as an optimal regime. However, keep a look-out that the bigger fishes are not getting all the food and feed strategically so that some gets swirled around the tank where shy customers may be waiting to get at it. As long as it is all cleared up within 5–10 minutes as far as gross inspection shows, all is well and the smaller fishes should have had their share.

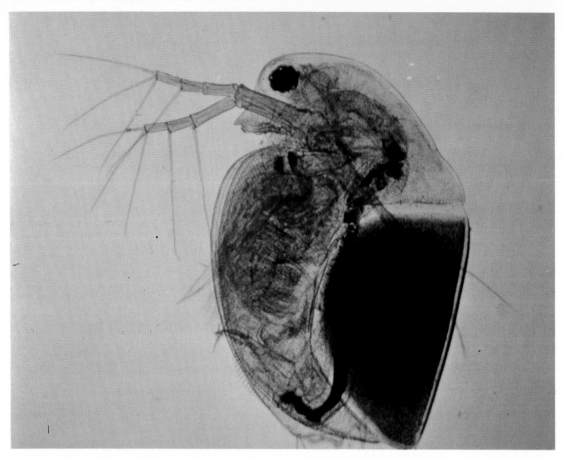

An enlarged photograph of a water flea (*Daphnia*). Watching the female *Daphnia* give birth to its young is fascinating. Photo by Dr. K. Knaack.

In the southern parts of the United States the crayfish species *Procambarus acutus* is sold principally for human consumption. In other areas it is utilized as live food for large fishes and other animals. Photo by Dr. H.R. Axelrod.

This sample of marine plankton consists mostly of crustaceans, an annelid, a small mollusk and some plants. Photo by K. Gillett.

A very young individual of *Tridacna gigas*, the giant clam, which can grow to weigh several hundred pounds. Smaller species of *Tridacna* generally have more colorful mantles. Photo by G. Marcuse.

FEEDING INVERTEBRATES

Some invertebrates, such as small crabs, shrimps and some univalve mollusks can be regarded as scavengers in the aquarium, and equivalent to snails in the fresh-water tank. Others need special attention so that they receive an adequate diet. Feeders on small particulate or living matter, the filter feeders and their allies, need quite frequent supplies of suspended fine food, whether living or dead, and usually need brisk stirring of the water to help distribute the food. An invertebrate tank is the better for strong currents anyway, which will carry even large particles to corals, small anemones and similar sessile creatures. Thus a good swirling tank which carries anything up to the size of adult brine shrimp around the scenery and gives every chance for the picking up of food is needed, at least at the time food is supplied and for some little time afterwards. The best method of producing this is strong aeration and an undergravel filter as the normal method of biological filtration. A protein skim-

ming device with ozone can be included, as it will not filter off much particulate matter, although if left on all the time it may kill some of the live food which passes through it.

Experience will tell how much to feed the filter feeders. Too little, and they will languish; too much, and pollution will start to show up. Here is where a good undergravel filter is so essential, as it will take care of minor pollution as long as overfeeding is not continued for long. So don't panic if your tank smells a bit in the experimental stages, just stop feeding as much for a day or two, perhaps turn up the ozone, and the smell should go. If it doesn't, start looking for something which has died if you cannot account visibly for all the inhabitants. Once or twice daily feeding for the filter feeders is enough, in the course of which other small creatures will also benefit.

Large anemones, crabs, lobsters, octopuses and some starfish need individual feeding. The anemones should have chunks of scallop, prawn

The red anemone *Actinia equina* can be kept in good condition with a sufficient diet of live fish, shrimp, crab and other invertebrates. Photo by A. Holtmann.

or other animal material dumped once or more weekly onto their expanded tentacles. Do not try to feed them if they are closed up or only half open. The others should be offered similar tidbits so that they do not unduly hunt around and kill something else for food. However, there are some incompatibilities, which means that many starfish and mollusks, particularly bivalves, do not mix, as the starfish will close over the mollusks and devour them. Octopuses and small crabs likewise, are not compatible, nor are carnivorous mollusks such as whelk or cone shells and many other mollusks upon which they feed. Sand filterers such as many worms and echinoderms other than starfish, are not going to be very happy in an aquarium with large particle gravel. Nudibranch mollusks, despite their beauty, are dubious starters since many are specialist feeders and we don't even know what they eat in some cases. Others are happy browsing on algae and so may settle down to a long existence in the tank. Some are even liable to appear from nowhere since a larval form may find sustenance and grow up from unnoticed origins. The same applies to occasional sponge or anemone growths, although no record seems to have appeared of

a coral growing spontaneously in the marine aquarium.

If you are sufficiently brave to be keeping fishes and invertebrates together, not very much needs to be added on the feeding front. A favorite experiment is anemones and anemone fishes. Some species of anemone fish definitely help to feed their anemones, taking larger pieces of food than they can eat themselves across to the anemone and thrusting them into the tentacles. Others seem to do this by accident, in that they retire to the anemone as a refuge, with a large mouthful of food which is too much to swallow and so they regurgitate or spit out part of it, to the anemone's benefit. Exactly the same fishes will also steal food from the anemone if you place it there in the first instance, so that there is two-way traffic. The writer has never seen an anemone fish lure another fish into the anemone, as is frequently asserted to be the case. However, only suitable species can be safely kept with large tropical anemones, as others will swim into the tentacles, getting killed or badly stung. Most wrasses, many *Dascyllus* species and lionfish are safe, the latter because they hit the anemone with the tips of spread fins or tail and very

Brittle stars such as this *Ophiocoma insularia* in their natural habitat subsist on small invertebrates found in the sea floor and rocks. Photo by A. Power.

Some cowries have been reported to somehow survive on nothing detectable as food for many months in a tank. Shown is *Cypraea histrio*. Photo by Dr. K. Knaack.

The genus *Periclimenes* encompasses a group of transparent beautifully colored shrimps with curious living habits. They are associated with sea anemones, corals and other invertebrates. Shown here are several of these shrimps among the tentacles of a sea anemone. Photo by Dr. H.R. Axelrod.

For a mollusk the octopus is very "intelligent." It can be taught to recognize shapes of objects and has been used much in invertebrate "psychology" studies. Photo by J.K. McCollum.

rarely suffer harm. On a rare occasion a lionfish has been seen to swim head-first into a *Stoichactus* anemone and suffer blindness afterwards. Small anemones and corals are no trouble in a reasonably sized tank.

There remain a few species of fish against which a special warning should be issued because they rarely feed adequately in captivity. Most specimens of the Regal or Royal Empress Angel (*Pygoplites diacanthus*) starve to death, so does *Chaetodon ornatissimus*. Some other chaetodons are difficult but most can be coaxed to eat something. Sea horses, pipefish, and the Mandarin fish (*Synchiropus splendidus*), are slow feeders, the first on live food only and the Mandarin on live or some prepared foods taken

from the bottom. With lively companions in the tank which rapidly eat up most or all of the food, these species will starve to death. Curiously the Psychedelic fish (*Synchiropus picturatus*) although a close relative of the Mandarin seems to be more aggressive and gets its share of food much more readily. Sea horses and lionfish, if the former are too big to be eaten by the latter, make a fine combination because they are interested in quite different sizes of live food and can be kept together in the same tank and fed adequately. While on the subject of lionfish, of all varieties, it should be realized that they eat shrimps, crabs and other crustacea quite readily, and are not safe with them.

Chapter 5

Diseases and Parasites

KEEPING FISHES HEALTHY

Our knowledge of the parasites and diseases of marine fishes is very patchy, and of cures is even patchier. Most of the treatments advocated are crude and frequently ineffective—hence the emphasis on keeping the fishes healthy rather than having to treat them frequently with medication of one sort or another. Regrettably, most marine aquarists will agree that this is not easy; despite having done everything right that we can think of, our collection will suddenly show signs of distress and then, on more careful inspection, may be seen to be suffering from an outbreak of *Oodinium* (velvet disease), or some other infection. Sometimes it is impossible to see how this has occurred, unless it has been latent in the tank and something unknown has started it up again.

There is no doubt that it is easier to treat a "sterile" system than a natural or biologically filtered one. In the sterile tank, there will usually be no invertebrates and no significant bacterial population to worry about. Depending on how it is aerated and filtered, it may or may not be necessary to turn part of the equipment off for a period during treatment, and the water can be cleaned up rapidly after treatment with such cures as copper or antibiotics, usually with activated charcoal. In the more biological set-up, with or without invertebrates, we have to worry about upsetting the bacterial action, the algal growth, and invertebrates if present. If we keep the filter going, the bacteria

may be killed; if we don't, they may die because of lack of circulating oxygenated water. However, despite fears and alarms expressed in the literature, the consequences of either line of action do not usually seem to be as serious as predicted, perhaps as long as the tank is large and not crowded and not stressed and has no invertebrates present. The filter may remove the medication too rapidly, however, which is another difficulty to be faced. This is illustrated in the case of copper treatment, in a diagram very freely based on some data of Dr. Miklosz, used merely to typify the sort of thing that happens. A useful hint is to try turning the biological filter on again for just a minute or so at a time, so as to get some oxygen to the bacterial every few hours without giving the filter long enough to extract much from the water. Unfortunately it is not always possible to arrange for this, when the filter may have to be left off and take its chance, or it may be turned down very low, if this is possible, so as to "tick over" gently without full action.

There are many differing views on the avoidance and treatment of fish diseases, just as there are with other animals, including humans! An advantage of a natural or semi-natural system is said by some to be that when all goes well, the fishes are healthier and do not get diseased readily, or even shed it if they do. It has been observed by some that even already diseased fish, infected with *Oodinium* or *Cryptocaryon*

A wrasse (*Bodianus anthioides*) photographed in a fish dealer's tank. Photo by Dr. H.R. Axelrod.

This long-snouted fish is *Lo vulpinus*, also commonly called foxface or just Lo. The species is apparently variable, with some forms having a black spot near the tail. Photo by G. Marcuse.

A yellow-tailed anemonefish, *Amphiprion clarkii*. For an anemonefish in captivity an anemone is not vital, but the anemone's presence provides greater security and a better natural hiding place than a piece of rock or coral. Photo by Dr. H.R. Axelrod.

An unfortunate event, a fish kill brought about by abnormal water conditions.

(marine white spot) may lose infection without passing it on to others. It has also been asserted that the fishes in such tanks unluckily get infected just as frequently as they do in sterile or invertebrate-free tanks, and that the association of clowns with their anemones does not free them of disease or prevent them from picking it up. These contradictory statements should not cause surprise; it may be that tank conditions were sufficiently different from one author to another to make them all true. The present writer has had such mixed experiences that it would obviously be foolish to be dogmatic, except on the point that we need to know a lot more before we can feel that we really understand many of the factors which control such events. It is no uncommon experience to find that shifting a fish from one aquarium to another can cure it of an infestation that resisted treatment in the original tank, or even that

shifting an apparently healthy fish to another tank with the same pH, specific gravity, temperature and nitrite values can nevertheless see the animal dead on the bottom within an hour. Why? We just don't know, unless it was *shock*, whatever that means.

So what do we do? First, we check regularly that everything *seems* to be going well. Periodic checks of pH, specific gravity and any other measures that we feel able to make should be part of the checking—say once per month, or anytime things seem to be going wrong. Daily checks of temperature, smell of the water (a very valuable guide), the look and behavior of all the fishes in the tank are mandatory. They don't take long and amply repay the trouble. Don't just glance at the fishes; look purposefully for fin conditions, any blemishes, odd swimming motions, hiding away in corners, and above all note whether each fish eats when fed. Failure of appetite in most marine fishes is a serious symptom that should never be ignored; if any fish shows it, give him a very careful look-over and watch him frequently from then on. Failure of appetite in a whole tank means that instant attention is needed and the cause identified if at all possible. Give a partial change of water at the earliest opportunity if you cannot see disease or diagnose any other potential cause, such as high ammonia or a temperature drop. The more crowded your tank and the smaller it is, the greater the necessity to act quickly.

QUARANTINE OF NEW FISHES

When treatment of newly received fishes was discussed earlier, it was from the point of view of equilibration of water quality, temperature and similar factors. If you have facilities for proper quarantine of new fish, which will not go into exhibition tanks until they have been observed and perhaps treated with medication, and until you are satisfied that all has been done to assure their healthiness that is possible, further steps are possible.

Some public aquaria routinely quarantine all new marine fishes and treat them simultaneously for certain potential diseases or parasites. Dempster reports that at the Steinhart Aquarium in San Francisco, all newly collected fishes are given formaldehyde treatment to relieve them of any flukes they may have. This treatment consists of a 1 hour bath in sea water with 1 ml of concentrated formaldehyde solution per gallon of water, every third day for 10 days. In the meantime they are kept in sea water with a concentration of 0.15 ± 0.03 ppm copper in the form of copper sulphate and citric acid (*sic*) for two weeks, to eradicate all external ciliates and flagellates. Others recommend potassium permanganate or other baths, with much the same end in view.

Keeping fish, either marine or fresh-water, in quarantine prior to distribution is good practice. Shown is the quarantine section for fishes collected by Pierre Brichard from Lake Tanganyika, Africa. Photo by Dr. H.R. Axelrod.

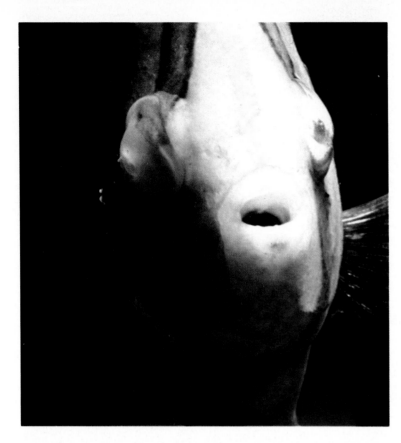

An ocellate butterfly fish, *Parachaetodon ocellatus,* with exophthalmic condition or pop-eye. Photo by Dr. H. Reichenbach-Klinke.

Note the total absence of any cloudiness in the eye of this young *Parachaetodon ocellatus*. Photo by Dr. H.R. Axel-rod.

An emperor angelfish, *Pomacanthus imperator* (bottom), photographed in the sea off Sri Lanka (Ceylon). In the wild state sick fishes are immediately disposed of by predators. A terribly diseased fish like the one illustrated here can only be seen in the confines of a tank. Top photo by Frickhinger, bottom photo by R. Jonklaas.

Note the small whitish elevated spot near the dorsal fin of this red clownfish, *Amphiprion frenatus*. It may be an indication of a site where some type of parasite is encysted. Photo by K. Paysan.

Unfortunately, not too many of us can devote separate aquaria to such treatment, and we should be able to rely on the dealer to quarantine and treat his fishes by such methods before passing them on for sale. If new fishes are added to an exhibition tank at quite infrequent intervals—which should of course be the case, or we are losing too many specimens—it is feasible to treat the tank with copper at each addition, to protect both the old and new fishes from outbreaks of at least such diseases as *Oodinium*. Some aquarists even add regular monthly doses of copper regardless, and report good results therefrom. It would not be feasible to catch out fishes and treat with formaldehyde prophylactically once they have been put into the show tank, as the upset caused in a decorated tank would probably be a greater risk than of flukes. The risk of flukes in fishes from a dealer is in the author's experience very low; they are too obvious to get overlooked even if he doesn't usually treat new fishes as a routine, and have probably been lost even before he gets them himself. This is one advantage of receiving fishes from a chain of handlers—collector and wholesaler and local dealer—and about the only one!

In the writer's experience, if fishes are going into a mixed invertebrate and fish tank, it pays to be as sure as possible of their freedom from disease before making the transfer. It is such a nuisance to have to catch them out again from the average exhibition tank, and even then not to know if the tank is by that time infected and so have to keep all fishes and invertebrates apart for a long period so that fish infections will die off before the fishes are introduced again. Alternatively, it would be necessary to remove all invertebrates and leave tank plus fishes to be treated, but then the invertebrates cannot always be easily moved or disinfected and so may well continue to harbor the disease, and we are back to square one. If the invertebrates are such as to be shifted without too great a risk of harm, treatment of them with an antibiotic will help to disinfect them and will not usually harm them. However, the breakdown products of many antibotics are toxic or inhibitory to algal growth, and should not be reintroduced with the invertebrates, or left in the exhibition tank without considerable change of water.

The seemingly best advice to the single tank man, or anyone without quarantine facilities is to treat with copper each time new fish are introduced as long as this is infrequently, and as long as the tank has fishes only. If keeping invertebrates with the fishes, make as sure as possible, that new arrivals are free of disease *before* putting them into your tank, which really means buy only from a dealer you can trust. Then offer up a few prayers in addition.

There has been a fad in animal husbandry for the prophylactic use of antibiotics in low dosage in the diet, found in some cases to increase weight gains and perhaps general health. It has spread to fish-keeping, with the result that some aquarists add small doses of

drugs at intervals to keep up a low "inhibitory" concentration. This may be right with copper, but it is dangerous to administer antibiotics in such a way, either in the water or the diet. First, there is evidence that if anything, fishes are harmed by such treatment and grow more slowly. This, however, is not the main danger. The second effect is that resistant strains of organisms will rapidly grow up and need higher and higher doses to kill them, or a switch to a different treatment. Highly resistant strains may develop which may be spread elsewhere with devastating results. A third effect has already been mentioned— potential damage to biological filters and the failure of the system to cope with wastes, hence poisoning of the fishes with ammonia, nitrites and other waste products. Use antibiotics for a specific purpose and then in adequate dosage.

The batfish *Platax teira* is a good community fish, but its fins can be damaged by fin nippers. It should be housed in a large tank together with mild-tempered fishes only. Photo by J.M. Bellantoni.

Red tube sponge. Photo by A. Power.

On account of the bright colors of some sponges one may be tempted to bring them home with the hope of keeping them in a tank. This is not recommended, because sponges usually harbor a great number of small invertebrates which can pollute the water as they die in the tank.

Vase sponge. Photo by A. Power.

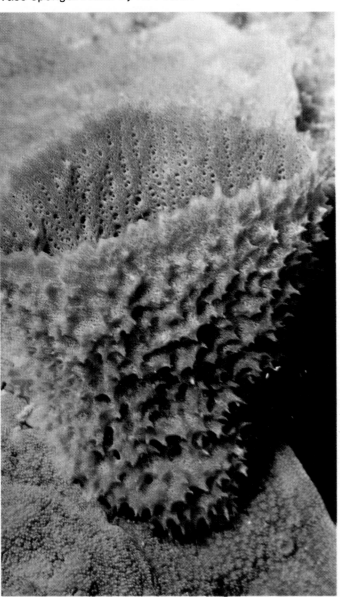

Branching orange sponge. Photo by D.L. Savitt and R.B. Silver.

A moonfish, *Monodactylus sebae*, with some myxosporidian parasite (*Henneguya*) cysts on the fins. Photo by Frickhinger.

Appearance of the tail region of a fish with white spot disease. Photo by Dr. G. Schubert.

SPECIFIC DISEASES

There does not seem to be much point in listing all the known important diseases of marine fishes, many of which have only been described from public aquaria or the sea itself. Those which tend to infest aquarists' tanks are rather restricted, at least as far as recognition goes, and tend to be spread within the trade, one suspects, rather than to be present very frequently on newly caught specimens. This is only a guess however. Thus, there are many diseases and parasites which depend on cycles, in nature, which do not lend themselves very fortunately to replication in the aquarium. Many flukes go through cycles of more than one host, so that both must be present if they are to reproduce. Nevertheless, other diseases are kept to a minimum in the sea because of a great dilution effect—the infective organisms released from a sick fish are scattered into millions of gallons of surrounding water, where-

as in the aquarium they find another host very rapidly and tend to infect him heavily straight away. For these reasons, the relatively few recognized diseases of marines will be described in approximate order of importance and recommended methods of treatment will be discussed.

VELVET DISEASE

This is related to the well-known fresh-water pest, *Oodinium limneticum* and other species, having as far as is known a similar life history. The usual causative agent in the marine tank would appear to be *Amyloodinium ocellatum* (Brown), but there is little doubt that there are other, related species which infest marine fishes. It is a dinoflagellate, a ciliated protozoan (one-celled animal) which infests the gills and outer surfaces of the fish, and in a heavy infestation is visible as a whitish powder-like dusting over the surface of the victim (the corresponding most common fresh-water species has a yellow color, not white). It is very difficult to see unless in a proper light, and is easiest to detect on black or dark surfaces, and when the body of the fish is facing you with an oblique lighting from above or the side. However, it is essentially a gill disease in marine fishes, and may be doing harm without visibility at all. Clown fishes (*Amphiprion*, *Premnas*, etc.) are particularly prone to surface infestation with *Amyloodinium* and may show it profusely without much in the way of other symptoms, while their tank mates may be badly affected and even dying. It always pays therefore to check these species as a valuable indication of potential trouble.

Usually, affected fishes have increased respiration (gill movements), scratch against rocks and other surfaces in the tank, have clamped fins and may show a wobbling motion, rather like swimming without getting anywhere, also characteristic of clown fishes in a perfectly healthy state when disturbed or in new surroundings. Some of these symptoms are also seen in fishes subjected to toxic water or to chilling, so that checks should be made to rule these out as possible causes, and all fish in the tank should be carefully scrutinized for the presence of velvet. If it cannot be seen, but a part change of water does no good, treat as though it is present.

Velvet disease goes through a life cycle in which free swimming dinospores settled onto surfaces of the fish and adhere, at first by their flagella, but later by a more active penetration of the outer layers of gill filaments or skin. The gills are preferentially infected presumably because they filter the organism from the water and offer a richly oxygenated surface for its adhesion and growth. Only when the water is loaded with dinospores will sufficient numbers settle onto the skin to be noticed. The heavily loaded gills become inflamed and irritable, and eventually unable to absorb sufficient oxygen, hence the scratching and

Clouded eyes and sunken belly are good indications that this saltwater catfish (*Plotosus anguillaris*) is not doing well. Photo by Dr. Herbert R. Axelrod.

A healthy surgeon-fish, *Zebrasoma desjardinii*, photographed in a dealer's display tank. Photo by Dr. Herbert R. Axelrod.

A *Zebrasoma desjardinii* individual with lateral line disease. The author has seen the same type of illness in one of his tanks; it affected only his angelfishes, and for months it attacked any new angel introduced. Photo by Dr. Herbert R. Axelrod.

A greatly enlarged photograph of a well-known cleaner shrimp, *Stenopus hispidus*. This shrimp is very much in demand by marine hobbyists. Photo by Dr. K. Knaack.

Life cycle of *Oodinium*:
the dinospores released
from the cysts in the
substratum infest the
fishes, grow and become
adult; the mature parasites
then fall to the bottom and
form cysts.
(From Amlacher.)

rapid, heavy respiration. There seems to be a referral of the sensation of irritation from the gills to the nose of the fish, which is what it scratches. Once firmly in the tissues, the dinospores grow and are eventually shed. According to some accounts they give rise to several hundred new organisms while on the fish and burst on shedding to free these new generation dinospores into the water. According to others they sink on leaving the fish to the bottom of the tank and there undergo multiplication, eventually to shed their offspring. To the aquarist, it doesn't much matter which is true; the end result is the same. The cycle appears to take up to about 10 days in the tropical tank, so that a new wave of infestation may well occur if treatment is not continued for such a period. High temperatures hasten the process, but do not seem to affect it otherwise.

As soon as velvet is known or suspected to be the cause of trouble, treatment should not be delayed. Despite there being a number of successful fresh-water cures, only one method of treatment can be fully recommended in the marine tank—*copper.* The use of copper seems a

crude and ancient type of treatment, but the fact remains that the majority of aquarists find it more successful than anything else. It is also successful against some other types of surface infestation, as we shall see later. It has to be used with care, as copper is highly toxic to fishes themselves in doses not much higher than are needed to cure the disease, but luckily marines are in general not so susceptible to copper poisoning as are fresh-water fishes; some species are, but most are not. Copper is also toxic to algae, and may kill the algal coating on rocks and coral if given in full dosage, so that if there is abundance of algae when heavy copper treatment is contemplated, remove much of it first, or it may die off and poison the tank. Copper acts in at least two ways. While it is said that it is of little use against the parasite while it is embedded in the host, it kills the free-swimming dinospore. It also causes copious mucus secretion by the gills and skin, and this helps to protect the fish from further infestation. It *may* also help to shed the parasites; certainly the rate of their disappearance is often suggestive of this, as they may be gone from the skin within a day or two of treatment, yet not all could have been ready to leave so rapidly.

The dosage and method of dosage of copper has been the subject of wide differences of opinion. The main limiting factor is toxicity to the fishes. In fresh-water, limits of about 0.15 to 0.33 ppm have been found for young fishes, but in marine tanks it appears safe below about 0.4 ppm. Some fish can take up to 0.8 ppm. The length of time of exposure is also important. Short periods of high dosage are no more toxic than long periods of lower dosage— hence Dempster's recommendation of 0.15 $\pm$ 0.03 ppm for continuous treatment for 2 weeks. Remember that unless filtration is turned off in an aquarium, copper concentrations are liable to fall rapidly, while to keep filters off for long periods is in itself dangerous. Dempster's quarantine arrangements must be such that

the copper ion concentration is maintained in an unfiltered (or non-carbon, non-biologically filtered) tank or by continuous drip or injection to a flowing system. Luckily, short pulses of high copper concentration or long periods of more constant lower concentration appear both to be effective. The former is what will tend to occur in ordinary administration to the single tank, not receiving a flow of outside water.

The form in which copper is given is also important. If we wish to achieve 0.4 ppm of Cu^{++} ions, we must give 2.0 ppm of $CuSO_4$ $\cdot 5H_2O$, the ordinary blue crystals of copper sulphate. This is 2 mg per liter, or approximately 7 mg per US gallon (9 mg per imperial gallon.) Thus 0.7 ml (or 0.9 ml) per gallon respectively of a 1% solution of copper sulphate will be the correct dosage. If we wish to achieve a dosage of 0.15 ppm, the amounts are

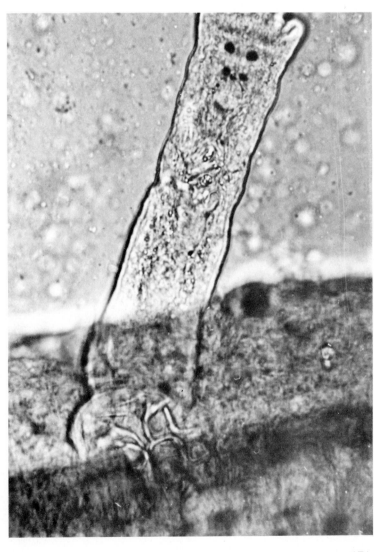

A monogenetic trematode (*Dactylogyrus*) feeding on the gills of a fish. The epidermal cells are eaten by the parasite. Photo by G. Schubert.

The dorsal spines of the stonefish *Synanceja verrucosa* carry a venom which can cause great pain and sometimes death to persons sensitive to the poison. Photo by Alimenta-Brussels.

The textile cone shell, *Conus textile,* should be handled with great caution because cone shells are apt to shoot out harpoon-like darts accompanied with a squirt of poison. Some deaths have been reported from cone bites. Photo by K. Gillett.

Hapalochlaena maculosa, the blue-ringed octopus, is known on the Australian coast as the culprit in some beach fatalities. These cephalopods are attractive, and people tend to pick them up without realizing their dangerous nature. Photo by W. Deas.

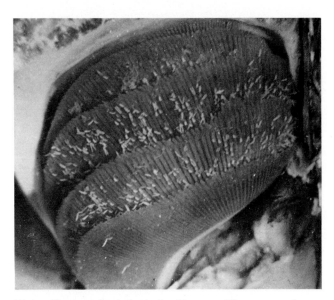
Fish gills heavily infested with parasitic copepods.

reduced to 0.26 ml (and 0.34 ml) per gallon. Copper citrate, or citric acid added to copper sulphate, has been recommended, also by Dempster, as being more soluble in sea-water, but this is debatable, as the end product in the complex of salts must be much the same. Certainly, when $CuSO_4 \cdot 5H_2O$ is made up in distilled water, as it should be, and added to the tank, there is an immediate fine cloudy precipitate, but this redissolves as it swirls around the tank. Copper complexes (salts of copper) together with chelating compounds (chemicals which seize onto heavy metals and sometimes alter their solubility and chemical reactivity) are also advocated as being more stable and less toxic than copper sulphate. In the experience of the writer they are poorly effective in the recommended dosage and equally toxic at equivalent dosages to copper sulphate.

How therefore to give copper treatment? Use a 1% copper sulphate solution at 1 ml per 4 US gallons in a sterile system, where it may not be rapidly removed, turning off any carbon filters or ion exchange resin filters for the duration of treatment. If possible, measure the amount of copper present each day as a guide to further action. If not, do not add more copper for at least several days unless the treatment is manifestly unsuccessful, in which case add another dose. Turn on the carbon filter or use an ion exchange resin such as Zeolite 225 for rapid removal of the copper if necessary.

Signs of excess dosage are fishes turning on their sides, gasping, and on prolonged exposure, exophthalmos (pop-eye). In a biological filtration system, turn off any carbon filters *unless* these are by now biological filters, turn down or use the biological filter periodically so as to minimize the extraction of copper while maintaining the integrity of the system, and add 0.7 ml per US gallon of the 1% copper sulphate solution (or for extreme precaution, two successive doses two days apart of 0.35 ml per gallon.) Measure consequent copper concentrations as before if possible and act accordingly to keep up about 0.15 ppm when a sufficient fall occurs. Often, symptoms disappear within a few days, and if medication is stopped, which is perhaps unwise, keep a very sharp look-out for a further outbreak.

WHITE SPOT

The marine version of fresh-water white spot disease (Ich) is also caused by a protozoan, *Cryptocaryon irritans*. Its life history is very similar to the fresh-water *Ichthyophthirius multifiliis*, and thus to that of velvet disease, in that free-swimming parasites attach themselves to the gills and skin, with a predilection for the gills in light infestations. Here they dig rather deeper than the *Oodinium* dinospores, and form much larger and more obvious cysts. These again drop off eventually and fall to the bottom of the tank, there to release a further generation of free swimming forms.

Cryptocaryon is found in the wild, but usually only as a light infection which causes little trouble. The infection is often present, as is velvet, in healthy looking fishes and can be brought on as a severe outbreak by chilling or other adverse treatments. The weakened fishes then succumb to a massive infestation resulting from multiplication within the tank and a lowered resistance to the free-swimming forms. Behavioral symptoms are very similar to those of fishes infected with velvet disease, and a differential diagnosis depends on careful observations of the spots—which are larger, deeper seated but still protuberant from the body or fin surface, and do not usually disappear very rapidly when treatment is given.

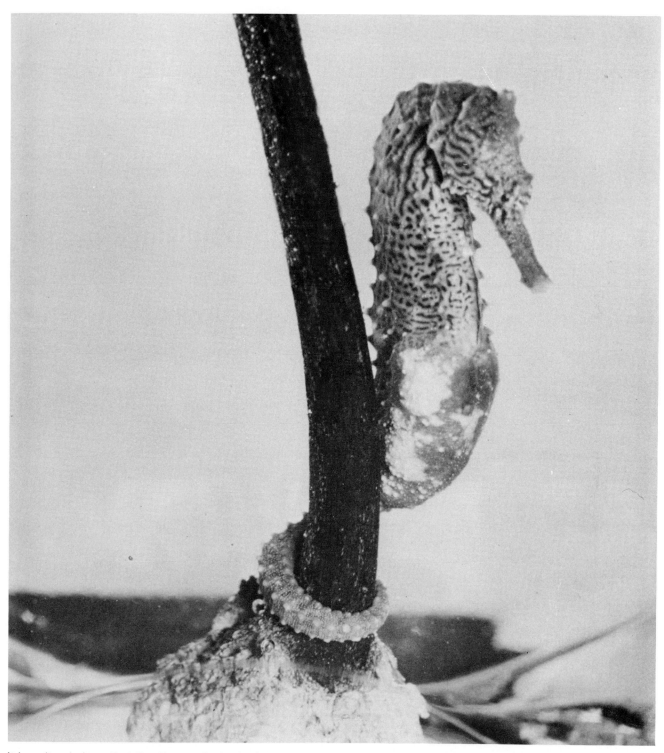

It is quite obvious that the diseased pouch of this male seahorse (*Hippocampus*) is not a healthy place for any young to develop. Photo by R. Straughan.

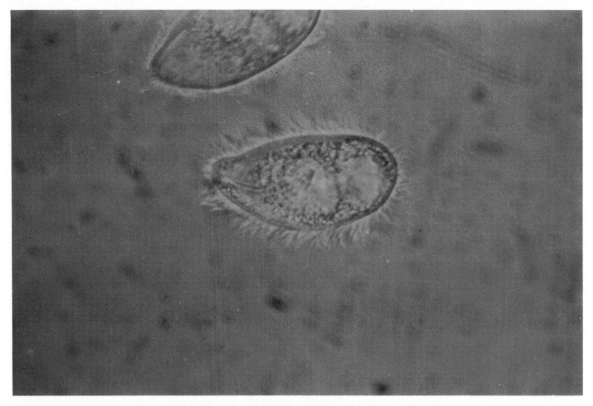

Cryptocaryon irritans is the marine counterpart of white spot disease. Shown are some parasites in the infective stage, when they are able to swim and infect new hosts. Photo by Dr. R.F. Nigrelli and Dr. G.D. Ruggieri.

Encysted stage of *Cryptocaryon irritans*. The parasite is seen lodged between the gill filaments. Photo by Dr. R.F. Nigrelli and Dr. G.D. Ruggieri.

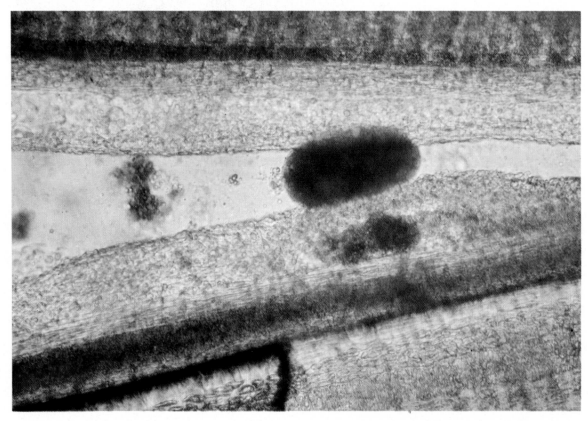

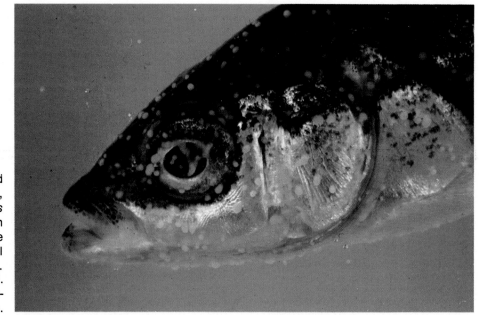

A three-spined stickleback, *Gasterosteus aculeatus*, with cysts of white spot disease all over its body. Photo by Dr. H. Reichenbach-Klinke.

Cells of *Ichthyophthirius multifilis* embedded in the fins under high magnification. Photo by Frickhinger.

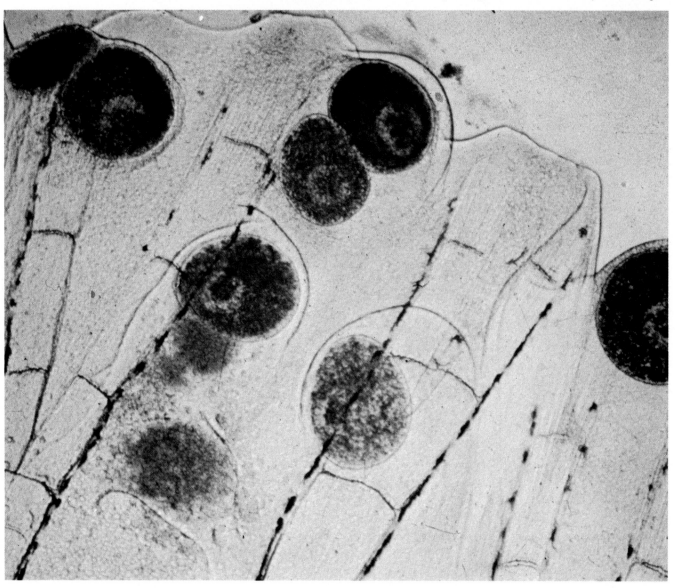

Butterflyfish (*Chaetodon collare*) being cleaned by a cleaner wrasse (*Labroides dimidiatus*). Take care not to introduce the mimic *Aspidontus taeniatus*, a blenny that nips scales of the fish instead of cleaning them. Photo by H. Hansen.

Both white spot and velvet are highly contagious and every care must be taken to handle an attack very cautiously. All nets and other equipment should be sterilized with boiling water or disinfectant before being used elsewhere, and splash or other contamination of one tank by another avoided. Outbreaks can result from new fishes carrying the diseases, from a weakened condition causing activation of a dormant infection in established stock, or from new, weakened fishes catching them from older residents and then passing the diseases back to the originators.

White spot is also treated with copper, by exactly the same methods as described for velvet disease. It thus doesn't really matter which condition the fish are suffering from as long as copper is to be used for treatment. However, other treatments than copper are more successful with white spot than with velvet, and may be given if you are satisfied that the disease is indeed white spot and *not* velvet. Thus, a treatment feasible in the presence of invertebrates is sodium sulphathiazole, or plain sulphathiazole if the more soluble sodium salt is not available. Use 1 level teaspoon (4ml) of the powder per 5 gallons (US) of aquarium water or per 4 gallons (UK). Dissolve or suspend the powder in a glass of fresh water before adding it to the aquarium and stir it up a bit if possible. In some hands, sulphathiazole seems to be very effective, but the concensus of opinion would seem to be that copper is quicker and surer.

Antibiotics also seem to be more effective against white spot than velvet, but not outstandingly reliable in either case. Both diseases are caused by protozoa, which are not in general susceptible to antibiotics. The wide-spectrum antibiotics such as aureomycin, chloromycetin and ampicillin (one of the newer wide-spectrum penicillins) are suitable for many bacterial infections, discussed later, but even these are less generally effective in marine aquaria than in fresh-water tanks. The reasons for this are obscure. Perhaps they break down or are inactivated more rapidly. No useful studies seem to have been made. Certainly some tetracycline derivatives, including aureomycin, rapidly color the water, even turning deep red overnight and causing severe cloudiness as well.

Note that one cannot detect any abrasions on this pair of *Heniochus acuminatus*. Skin abrasions from whatever cause are potential sites for bacterial and fungal infections. A damaged integument also reduces the fish's protection against the invasion of parasites. Photo by K. Paysan.

The cleaner wrasse *Labroides dimidiatus* should still be fed regularly, because the opportunity to pick off parasites from other fishes is not present in captivity. Photo by Dr. Herbert R. Axelrod.

Amyloodinium ocellatum cells in various stages of growth in the gills. The parasite at this stage is not identifiable as a flagellate. They are responsible for marine velvet disease. Photo by Frickhinger.

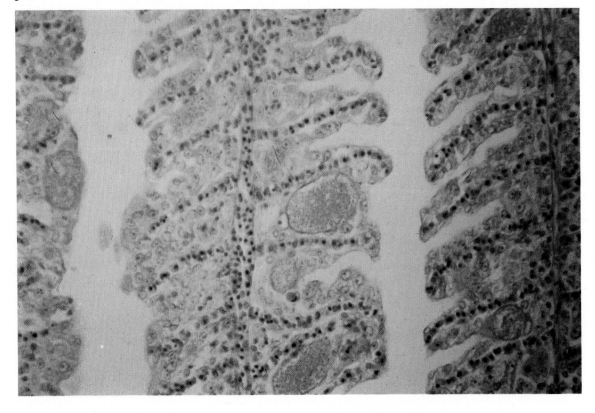

Skin lesions on
a rock bass with
tuberculosis.

Neon tetras,
*Paracheirodon
innesi*, all
victims of
tuberculosis.
Loss of
pigments and
fin damage are
very evident.

Spinal curvature
in these
guppies,
*Poecilia
reticulata,* was
traced to tuber-
culosis
infection later.

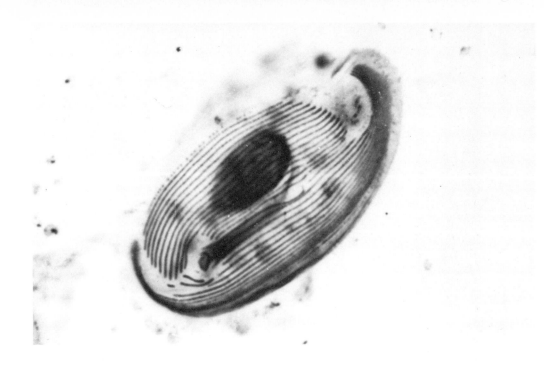

Brooklynella hostilis is a parasitic ciliate of marine fish similar to *Chilodinella,* which attacks fresh-water fishes. Photo by Dr. Lom.

BACTERIAL DISEASES

As with higher vertebrates, bacterial infections in fishes are very varied and frequent, but as far as the marine aquarium is concerned, discussion will be mostly confined to those with external manifestations such as so-called fin rot, tail rot, mouth fungus (which is not fungal in origin), ulcers, etc. Others causing pop-eye or other obvious symptoms such as hollow belly or general wasting are internal rather than otherwise, but the obviousness of the symptoms alerts us and calls for treatment. It will not be supposed that a pathological examination will be possible; these are more appropriate to hatchery conditions or to epidemics in public aquaria, where many fishes are in danger and the expertise to try to stop an outbreak is likely to be available. In the private aquarium a dead fish tends to be one in which we lose interest! Also, by the time a causative organism may have been identified, the disease is likely to have run its course, usually killing susceptible specimens, or been halted by hit or miss methods. In a marine tank, events usually happen fast and there may be no time for proper diagnosis.

Inflammation and erosion of fins and tail have been attributed to many different types of causative organism, particularly *Pseudomonas, Aeromonas,* and *Haemophilus* species of bacteria. Such conditions are not frequent in the wild, but occur in captivity. Mouth fungus, which may also attack fins, tail and body, is attributed in fresh-water fishes to *Chondrococcus columnaris* and *Cytophaga columnaris,* but it is not clear whether the marine varieties are caused by the same bacteria. The mouth is inflamed and cotton-wool-like tufts of bacteria protrude from it. The fish affected is obviously in difficulty when it tries to eat, and may die from starvation as much as directly from the infection. The best treatment is one of the wide-spectrum antibiotics, which may be administered in the food, or less advisedly, added to the tank water. Of the common antibiotics, chloromycetin seems to be the most useful in the marine aquarium, least toxic and also colorless. Although it tastes very bitter to us, fishes don't seem to object to it and will readily eat their usual diet mixed with the antibiotic. Somewhere between 0.1% and 1% of antibiotic in the diet is usually recommended. In view of possible losses enroute, the higher figure seems advisable. The powdered antibiotic can be added to dry or flake food, and will usually adhere long enough for much of it to be eaten before it falls away or dissolves in the water, or it can be incorporated into mixtures of prawn, scallop, etc., with much the same result. This technique of administration seems more often successful than dosage to the whole tank, it uses very much less antibiotic, and it does not present problems of effects on biological filters, algae, or cause significant water pollution.

If it is desired to treat the whole tank, quite high doses are needed, higher in general than one would expect from the blood levels of the drugs concerned that are achieved in normal therapy. Recommendations vary from about 50 mg to 1g per US gallon (3.6 liters) of aquarium water. The author feels that 50 to 100 mg should usually be sufficient, but there are many accounts of much higher amounts being needed—a reflection of the rather strange ineffectiveness of antibiotics in the marine tank. If chloromycetin is used, there is no need to change the water, unless algal growth appears to be persistently depressed, when it is a good idea to add sufficient new water to enable it to continue; about 50% change usually seems adequate. Various sulphonamides have also been used against bacterial diseases, in similar dosages to that recommended for sulphathiazole in white spot disease. Their use would not appear to be any more effective in general than that of antibiotics, but they can also be mixed with the food up to about 1% by weight,

a treatment said to be especially effective against mouth fungus.

TUBERCULOSIS

Also a bacterial disease, tuberculosis falls into the second class to be discussed—a disease of the internal organs with obvious general effects. Affected fish are emaciated and may show necrosis of fins and of course of internal organs. They are usually of very poor color and may show skin lesions as well as fin and tail lesions. It is thought that piscine (fish) tuberculosis only becomes a problem in fishes already weakened from other causes. The disease is thus of low-grade infectivity, but may become a serious problem if untreated, and if the predisposing causes are not corrected. It is not a rapid killer, and may therefore be diagnosed within a useful period with time to save other tank mates from the same fate. It is caused by one species or another of *Mycobacterium*. In the marine aquarium, *M. marinum* or *M. kansasi*, which are possibly variants of each other,

A juvenile angelfish (*Pomacanthus semicirculatus* with some lesions in the facial area. Unless a disease is known, the success of a specific treatment is a matter of chance. Photo by G. Marcuse.

The cleaner wrasse *Labroides dimidiatus* cleans not only the skin and fins of a fish but also the gills and mouth cavity. Apparently the fish being cleaned, an angelfish (*Pomacanthus semicirculatus*) welcomes this activity. Photo by M. Goto.

A cleaner wrasse emerging from the mouth of a painted sweetlips, *Spilotichthys pictus*. Some fishes are reported to actively solicit the attention of cleaners. Photo by A. Power.

A collector transferring a *Diodon* from a collecting basket into a bucket. Gloves protect the handler from injury from the spines of the fish. Good collectors do not use harmful chemicals to stun or immobilize the fish. Photo by R. Jonklaas.

would appear to be the commonest species. A note of warning—*M. kansasi* is found in human wounds and there is a possibility of infection, perhaps rather remote. The diagnostic features are acid-fast, non-motile, Gram-positive rods, yellow in color when grown on glycerol-agar. Since fishes tend to attack and eat parts of sick comrades, and to eat corpses left in the tank, probably the greatest danger threatening a collection when some members are suffering from tuberculosis is transfer of the disease by direct infection from moribund specimens. So get rid of them and improve general conditions as rapidly as possible. Overcrowding, poor diet, underfiltration and hence toxic water are all potential causes of the infection getting a hold.

Treatment with antibiotics as for bacterial diseases in general is possible in light infections —far preferably by mixing with the food, as the disease is essentially internal. Kanamycin or tetracycline have been recommended.

LYMPHOCYSTIS

This is a virus disease in which large spots resembling pimples or boils extending to mulberry-like growths occur on the body and fins. They are composed of swollen connective tissue, and occur mostly on individual fishes rather than as an epidemic, especially initially. No specific cure is known, and as virus diseases are resistant to usual forms of treatment, it is best to get rid of infected specimens, or at least to improve conditions and perhaps install ozone or ultraviolet sterilization in the hope of killing the free virus particles. The same danger exists as with bacterial infections, that dead or dying fishes will be eaten or nibbled at and pass the disease on.

ICHTHYOSPORIDIUM (Ichthyophonus)

A fungal disease this time, *Ichthyosporidium gasterophilum*, which is the marine version of *I. hoferi* in fresh-water fishes, causes a primary infection in the liver and also, varying somewhat with species, in the kidneys, heart, brain, gills and eyes. Breakthrough to the exterior may occur, when the disease manifests itself as ulcers, skin hemorrhages, including dropsy-like swelling of the skin and scales. Infection takes place by the eating of the infected material, including other fishes or crustacea. Various forms of the fungus may be identified microscopically, and it seems that minute one-celled stages are found in the gastro-intestinal tract of the fish, which penetrate the gut wall and settle down, via the bloodstream, in various organs. There they encyst and grow rapidly and spread by releasing daughter cells which form adjacent cysts, until the area is necrotic and the host eventually dies. The process is often accompanied by pigmentation.

Early in this process, antibiotics may attack the parasite in the gut or as it penetrates the gut wall, but are later found to be ineffective. Feeding antibotics as above would then appear to offer the best chances of limiting spread of the disease and curing early infections.

FLUKES

These are trematode worms, of very many different species, which are parasitic on fishes. The seriously troublesome ones are in the group of monogenetic trematodes, needing no intermediate host or hosts and thus able to infect directly from fish to fish. The very numerous species of digenetic trematodes, which need to alternate between fish and other animals to complete their reproductive cycles, rarely find the necessary secondary host or hosts under aquarium conditions, but in mixed fish and invertebrate tanks, they could do so. A mollusk is very often the intermediate host, for example. The monogenetic trematodes, or Monogenea, are nearly always external parasites and infest gills, body and eyes and cause great irritation because of their attachment by sets of hooks.

The most important feature of this monogenetic trematode *Gyrodactylus* is the series of hooks on the head region. These hooks enable the fluke to cling tenaciously to the skin and gills of the host fish. Illustration by Dr. Herbert R. Axelrod.

A flounder with cysts of lymphocystis on the body and fins.

Close-up of several cysts on the flounder shown above.

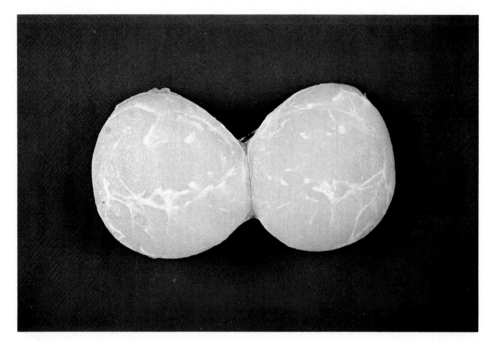

A benign tumor from the muscle of a large-mouth bass. Photo by Mawdesly-Thomas.

Epithelioma (cauliflower disease) on the head of an eel. A virus has been implicated but not proved as the cause of this disease.

They are sometimes species specific, particularly among the Pacific angelfishes, whereas the Atlantic angels are characteristically parasitized by flukes which are not choosy as regards their hosts. So one or two angels may be heavily infested in a community tank, with all the other fishes free or practically free of the flukes.

The treatment of choice is a formaldehyde bath, which necessitates removal of the affected fishes for a 1-hr. bath in salt-water containing 1 ml of concentrated formaldehyde per US gallon. A single treatment may be enough, but repeated treatments at 3-day intervals are usually recommended. This is obviously a nuisance, but it is useless to try copper or antibiotics with nearly all species of fluke, and dangerous to add effective amounts of formalin to the aquarium, unless the whole of the water can be flushed out and replaced within an hour. Sometimes, however, a mere change of water is enough. The author vividly recalls an experience of a short time ago when two angels and one *Dascyllus* in a 140 gallon tank were the only fishes affected out of about 30 in the tank, yet they were very heavily parasitized. They were removed for treatment to another empty but established tank with undergravel filtration, with the intention of seeing whether some other form of medication than formalin might work. On being left overnight without treatment, they shed their flukes, lost all signs of irritation and did not fall sick again. On being returned a week or so later to the original tank they did not become reinfected and all was well.

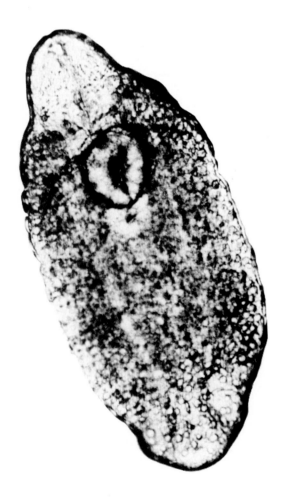

The digenetic fluke *Diplostomum spathaceum* can invade the eye and cause glaucoma in fish. This parasitic worm requires a snail intermediate host in order to complete its life cycle.

A bullhead (*Ictalurus*) that has succumbed to columnaris disease. This disease is very difficult to control except during the early stages. Photo by Davis.

The proboscis of a spiny-headed worm (*Acanthocephalus*) under high magnification shows the presence of rows of strong recurved hooks. These worms are generally found along the intestinal tract, but they also stay in the body cavity. Photo by Dr. E. Elkan.

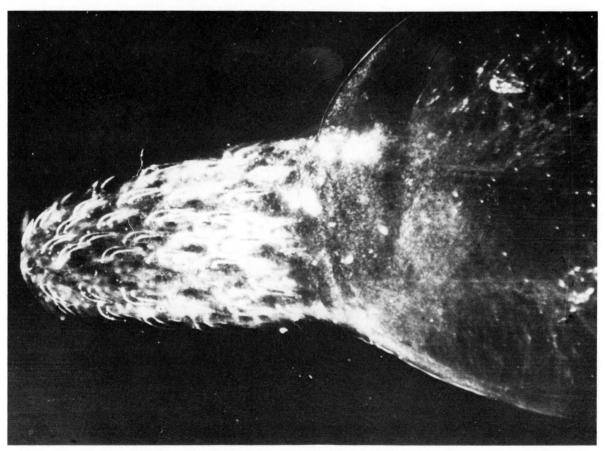

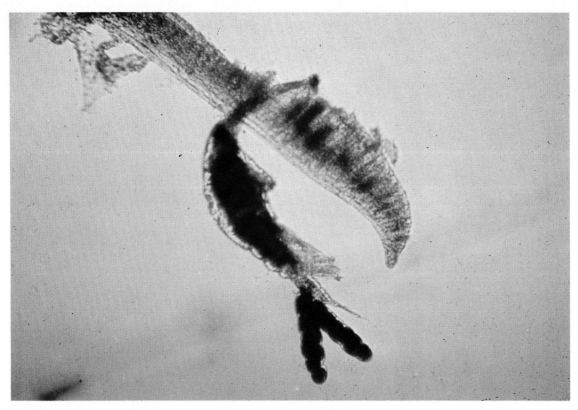

A gill copepod (*Ergasilus*) hanging on a gill filament of a white crappie. Photo by Dr. F. Meyer.

The monogenetic trematode of the genus *Tetraonchus* may be found in both marine and fresh-water fishes. They are found on the skin and gills. Photo by Frickhinger.

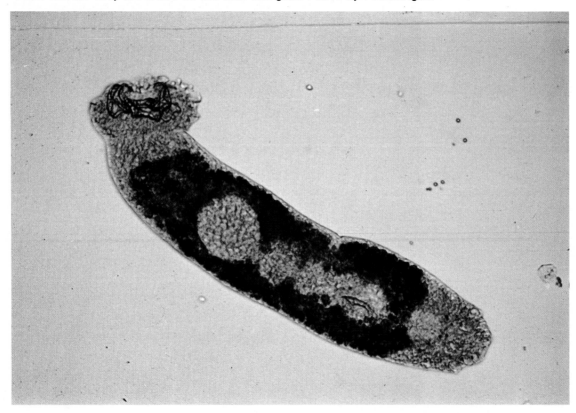

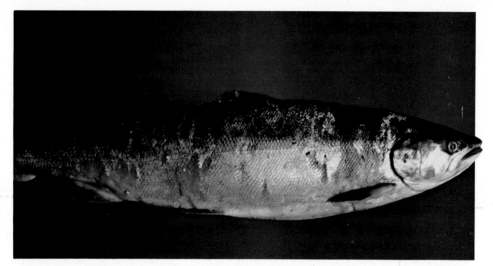

A salmonid fish with lesions caused by the bacterium *Aeromonas liquefasciens*.

Appearance of a lesion caused by vibrio disease, another bacterial infection, on a steelhead rainbow trout *Salmo gairdneri*.

An advanced case of bacterial tail rot in a cichlid.

Anemone stings are fatal to fishes, except anemonefishes that are apparently immune to the stinging cells. However, not all types of sea anemones kill fish for food. Photo courtesy of RKO Radio Pictures.

EXOPHTHALMOS (pop-eye)

This condition, in which the eyeballs protrude, sometimes alarmingly and with eventual loss of the eye, may be caused by a variety of conditions. When due to infection, it has been associated with bacterial, viral and fungal diseases, and if occurring during the course of such diseases it may disappear when they are treated. More frequently, it is associated with non-infective agencies, such as copper, other toxic substances, release of gas from the blood-stream, or even genetic causes exemplified by the telescope-eyed goldfishes. Interestingly, it can also be caused in the goldfish by administering thyroid-stimulating hormones which in humans cause the same condition. It is unusual for many fishes to be suffering from

exophthalmos in the same aquarium and the condition is not usually contagious. When it is of non-infective origin, recent aquarium history may suggest the cause. Has the tank been treated with copper or other potential cause, has it recently been overaerated or heated up (which may cause nitrogen to leave the blood-stream and form bubbles in regions like the eye)? It has been suggested that minute bubbles from a fine air-spray may actually get into the blood and settle in the eye. This is incredible, but high pressure water entering the tank, as in some public aquaria, may carry excess dissolved gases which will cause fine bubbles to form both in the water and in the fish.

194

When exophthalmos occurs as a result of gas bubbles (usually nitrogen, as with the "bends" in diving) it must be remembered that they have probably been forming elsewhere as well. In the nervous system they may cause abnormal behavior or paralysis, in the fine blood vessels they may cut off circulation and damage the heart, kidneys, etc. The best treatment is to lower temperature within the limits of safety, cut down any excessive aeration, particularly from any kind of pressure pump such as is needed to force the water through a fine filter capsule, and hope that any affected fishes may equilibrate before showing severe effects, whether exhibiting exophthalmos or not. If the eye eventually shows one or two single large bubbles, these may be extracted through a fine needle and hypodermic syringe, as they will take a long time to dissolve. However, the procedure is hazardous, but even if the eye is destroyed—either by the bubbles or attempts to remove them—fishes can regenerate an eye in some circumstances. This may sound rather incredible, but it is so.

TUMORS AND GROWTHS

Not all growths in fishes are of infective origin, and there are many varieties of cancer or tumor that have no known cure, some being genetic. They are not dangerous either, so if an isolated fish suffers from a visible growth that does not appear to be infective—usually, but not always, it will not behave as if discommoded by the growth unless the latter is very large—it may be left alone. If the fish appears to be worried by it or frankly in distress, or if the growth is unsightly, it is time to destroy the fish.

Many tumors are internal and will not be detected until they are very large or are causing severe damage. The fish is then best removed and painlessly killed. Liver tumors are frequent and often due to dietary deficiencies, as is fatty degeneration of the liver, which is not a tumor.

Exophthalmus can occur in both marine and freshwater fish. One of the eyes of this paradise fish (*Macropodus opercularis*) is completely out of the eye socket. Photo by R. Zukal.

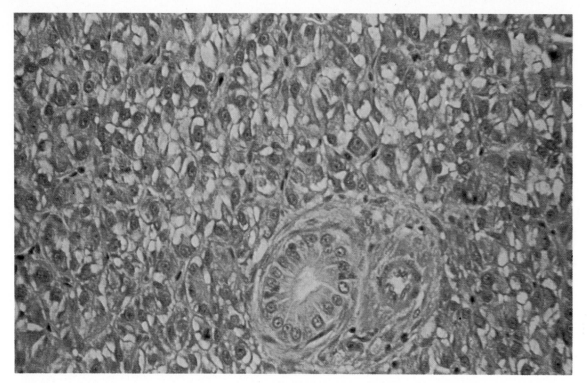

A section of the liver of a fish suffering from fatty degeneration which is a nutritional and non-infectious disease.

A culture of the bacteria *Aeromonas liquefasciens* especially prepared for photography with fluorescent light. Photo by D.H. Lewis.

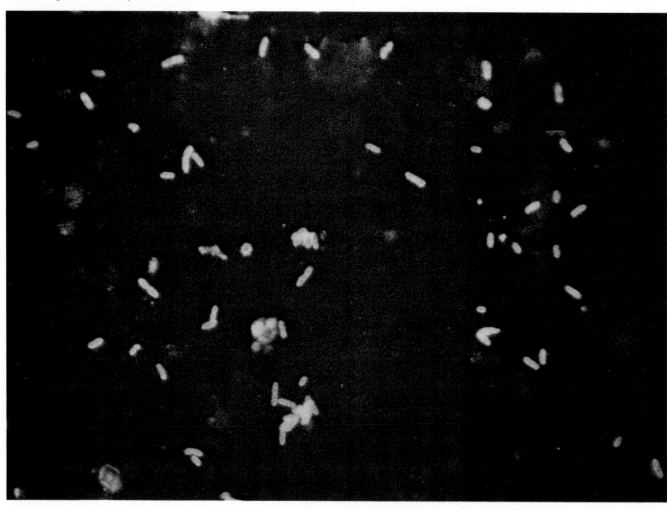

A haddock with fibroma. Note the enlarged scales on the tumor. Photo by Mawdesley-Thomas.

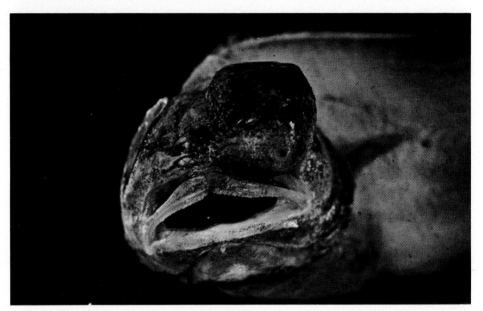

Parasitic cyst on the snout of a morid catfish. Photo by Mawdesley-Thomas.

A pair of whitefish (*Chondrosoma nasus*) showing the possible effects of water pollution.

197

TOXIC CONDITIONS

We have already studied the toxins of the nitrogen cycle, which are the main natural toxins to be expected in the fish tank (salt or fresh). There are many other toxic substances, mainly of external origin, which must be considered as potential causes of trouble in aquaria. They may be introduced in the water, air, or by materials placed in the tank as part of the equipment or decorations. If fishes look distressed and no definite signs of disease can be seen, poisoning must always be suspected and the possible cause carefully sought. It should be particularly suspected when the fishes stop feeding, show blotchiness or extreme pallor or deep coloration, or a peculiar appearance which makes them look as if they have rubbed themselves against a rough surface and lost some of the skin. A check of obvious causes of trouble such as pH changes, ammonia or nitrite build-up, extreme specific gravity readings or excess copper if used previously should be made, and if these are all in order, look carefully over all accessories for deterioration, exposed metal, breakdown of non-inert plastics and the like. Smell can sometimes be a guide. If the water does not smell right, which is only faintly of the usual marine or earthy odor, be guided as far as is possible by the nature of the smell. Fly sprays, new paint, heavy tobacco smoke, any other common spray such as hair, furniture or cleaning sprays may be a source of trouble, especially if sucked in by an air pump and passed into the water. A covered tank with the slight outward flow of air resulting from airlifts and airstones is safe as long as incoming air is clean.

Tubifex worms can be a possible source of phenolic poisoning and of fatty degeneration. Photo by R.E. Gossington.

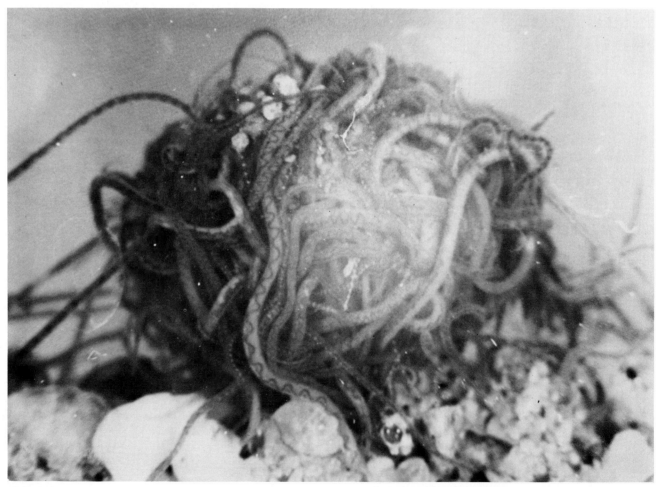

The blotchy condition of the skin of this angelfish (*Pomacanthus semicirculatus*) is typical of that caused by poisoning or wrong conditions and not from bacterial origin. Photo by G. Senfft.

HOUSEHOLD MATERIALS

Soap, detergents, flakes of tobacco or many other materials under the nails are all dangerous. Always clean the hands before servicing aquaria, not merely by washing, but also by thorough rinsing in clean fresh-water. The same applies to anything to be immersed in the tank or to be used to convey food. The practice of allowing detergent-washed dishes to dry without thorough rinsing may not be good in the long run for ourselves, but it can be deadly to fishes, and a dangerous build-up of detergents can occur. These are not only poisonous in themselves, but they strip the fish of its protective layer of mucus, with the result that gill function is impaired, skin resistance is lower, and, for example, an anemone fish may be killed by its own anemone. Hard detergents are perhaps the worst, but the bio-degradable varieties are not safe either. The common benzosulphonates are toxic in quantities as low as a few parts per million, probably in fractions of a ppm when present over long periods of time.

Phenols, derived from oily or tarry materials contaminating water in which *Tubifex* has been gathered, have been found accumulated in the tissues of fishes, and have experimentally been found to have even greater toxicity in many cases than detergents. *Tubifex* should be fed sparingly and very carefully washed if there is any oiliness in the water where it is found. Phenols or cresols can also enter the aquarium in other ways—in food, poor cements or varnishes, or as breakdown products of cheap plastics.

Beware of moray eels like this *Gymnothorax flavimarginatus*, whose bite can lead to serious infection if left untreated. Size is not important, for even small morays can be very nasty. Photo by A. Power.

Equipped with powerful beak-like jaws, the sharpnosed puffer *Canthigaster valentini* can crunch coral rock while searching for food. Thus it can easily give anyone a painful bite if mishandled. Photo by M. Goto.

A tank with exposed metal parts like this rarely seen old fashioned aquarium is not suited for keeping marine fish. The chemical action of salt water on metal results in substances toxic to fish. Photo by Mervin F. Roberts.

METALLIC POISONING

Many observations of the concentrations of various metals poisonous to fresh-water fishes have been made, but very few for marine fishes. However, we must assume that similar toxicity in the marine tank holds, and that the particularly poisonous metals mercury, silver, zinc and cadmium should be strictly avoided. Don't use mercury thermometers in aquaria, for example, as, if one is broken, it can be a source of endless trouble. Copper has been dealt with, but one must remember that it is nearly as toxic as mercury and silver and that no casual introduction of copper should ever be allowed. Exposed metal surfaces—including stainless steel—are much more dangerous in the salt-water tank than in the fresh-water one because of the highly corrosive action of sea water. Drip-back from overhead fittings, creep of salt deposits around anything used as a cover or support around the top of the tank all spell potential danger.

GASES

The most dangerous gas in normal circumstances is chlorine which often occurs in lethal concentrations in tap water—0.2 ppm can kill in a few days. With the use of artificial mixes, as much care must be taken as for fresh-water aquaria, and enough time should be allowed for evaporation of the chlorine before adding new water to the tank. With aeration at room temperature, a day or two is sufficient. Chlorine

poisoning can be recognized by paleness and blotchiness of the skin, deep-sunk eyes, listlessness and weak respiration, which ends in cessation of gill movement and death.

Hydrogen sulphide (H_2S) is a toxin produced by anaerobic breakdown of organic materials such as occurs when thick sand is not aerated, or an undergravel filter is left off too long. It smells of rotten eggs. The gas combines with the hemoglobin in the blood and prevents it from carrying oxygen. (So does carbon monoxide, the poisonous gas in domestic gas supplies and car exhaust fumes). Less than 1 ppm of H_2S is toxic and so it is a potent killer in a tank that is "going bad."

Carbon dioxide (CO_2), although in itself poisonous in high doses, is almost never a problem unless aeration breaks down, when lack of oxygen together with CO_2 accumulation leads to trouble, unless the tank is very understocked. The fishes show gasping respiration, irregular respiration, ending with asphyxia and paralysis. Dependence on oxygen concentration varies with species, but nearly all marine fishes are more sensitive to oxygen lack than fresh-water species. Curiously, excessive oxygen concentration can be toxic, as when supersaturation of the water occurs because of algal O_2 production, in bright light or the jetting of high pressure water into the aquarium.

A male clownfish *Amphiprion ocellaris* fanning its nest. This species is known to spawn even in small tanks although the rearing of the young to maturity would require much more attention and time than most hobbyists can normally give. Photo by Dr. J. Meulengracht-Madsen.

Too much aeration may be mechanically as well as physiologically harmful. Strong currents can present swimming difficulties and supersaturation with oxygen may be toxic to the fish. A weak swimmer like this trunkfish (*Tetrasomus gibbosus*) can be harmed by violent aeration. Photo by G. Marcuse.

A parrotfish photographed in the reef inside a mucus cocoon. The cocoon provides the fish some protection during the night as it sleeps. Photo by M. Goto.

Index

Page numbers printed in **BOLD** face refer to illustrations and photographs.